Our Life

Becoming a Masterpiece in the Potter's Hands

MARY WHITE

ISBN 978-1-64670-780-5 (Paperback)
ISBN 978-1-64670-781-2 (Digital)

Covenant Books, Inc.
11661 Hwy 707
Murrells Inlet, SC 29576
www.covenantbooks.com

Permissions Granted for Use

DEDICATION

*M*y precious sons, Brad and Chad, who have always been the center of my heart and love.

My lovely grandchildren Bradley, Abby, George, and Ruby, the young and young at heart, who love to dream and have touched my life in ways they'll never understand.

My loving daughter-in-law, Abigail, who also has always held a special place in my heart, admired and loved as a daughter.

It is my heartfelt desire that as you read through the pages of this book, you will find it to be an inspiration to your life and understand the depth of love from which it was written.

CONTENTS

UNFINISHED PORTRAIT

There are stories that touch our heart and bring us to the realization that although very flawed and imperfect, God views our life as His workmanship and what we can become in a way to glorify Him. He sees our life as children of promise in which He sees our inner beauty.

There is a story told about the thirty-second president of the United States, President Franklin D. Roosevelt. An artist, Madame Shoumatoff, was commissioned to paint "his" portrait. In the midst of the painting, President Roosevelt collapsed from a cerebral hemorrhage. Originally, this unfinished portrait was a watercolor likeness to portray a man of inner strength.

When compared to photographs that had been taken much earlier, they revealed a very different rendition of this national leader. Instead of strength, his expressions showed a man who was both physically and emotionally encumbered by the burdens of his leadership, one of which was the Great Depression.

When Madame Shoumatoff decided to resume the portrait, she decided the original watercolor portrait would not depict the man she chose to represent. Instead, she painted a portrait that showed his convictions and charm. The flaws that might have shown in the earlier portrait

9

were absent in the new portrait. In its place, the painting embodied a man of honesty, determination, and certitude that emulated the characteristics he portrayed during the worst economic crisis in US history. The final portrait of President Roosevelt was painted to represent a man's legacy in the eyes of the world for the difference he made.

Have you ever looked in the mirror and pondered over a true understanding of yourself or how others perceive you? In 1 Corinthians 13:12 (NLT), Paul reminds us, "Now we see things imperfectly, like puzzling reflections in a mirror, but then we will see everything with perfect clarity. All that I know now is partial and incomplete, but then I will know everything completely, just as God now knows me completely."

I often wonder what my portrait would reveal if depicted by an authentic and proficient artist—our Creator. Would it be a rendition of a person of strong character or dishonor, endurance or apathy, humility or arrogance, sincerity or hypocrisy? I often wonder what people truly see in me. I believe that each of us wants to be viewed as genuine, caring individuals, but I also believe that to some degree we hide behind a kind of veneer, hiding some of our imperfections from others. But I know that those flaws will be hidden only temporarily. A time will come that the true revelation of who we are will be complete. Just as Madame Shoumatoff painted the portrait of President Roosevelt for his inner beauty, God knows we are still growing and maturing.

As children of promise, God sees in each of us the promise and redemption that was won at the crucifixion of His Son at Calvary. Although we cannot see the finished portrait, He sees us fully and what we can become as a masterpiece of His design in a way to ultimately glorify Him: "We are His workmanship created in Christ Jesus for good works, which God prepared beforehand that we should walk in them" (Eph. 2:10).

As we journey through life in becoming the masterpiece He desires, we will experience challenges and troubles, experiencing pain, but each of these encounters will broaden our understanding of God's wisdom as He shapes us into the magnificent design of His plan. Solomon's spiritual insight led him to write, "Trust in the Lord with all your heart and do not lean on your understanding. In all your ways acknowledge Him, and He will make your paths straight. Do not be wise in your own eyes; fear the Lord and turn away from evil" (Prov. 3:5–7).

Through the eyes of others, we may appear irrational and a disappointment, but in the eyes of God, He knows what we were and what we can become. Stopping to look within myself, I began to reflect on my "original portrait," my life before I met Christ. With all my flaws, I realize He worked each disappointment to work all things in and through His glory. It was not His plan to free me from all pain and anguish, but to develop an intimate relationship with Him and prepare me for eternity. I know one thing for sure He sees me as His masterpiece, being molded, still in the process of becoming what He has planned. How refreshing it is to have the assurance that until I step into eternity, He will continue to shape and conform me into the image of His Son. Our journey, regardless of its length, must be viewed from an eternal perspective. We must never forget who we are and to Whom we belong. As children of our Heavenly Father, we have a divine worth and destiny. As we grow closer to Him, He will grow closer to us. The difficulty we face is our failure to surrender our will to Him.

Our gift to God is becoming His Masterpiece, and it is not immediate. It is a continual process as He transforms us along our journey through life, shaping us into the reflection of what He chooses us to be through His Son. Each step we take, one day at a time, we learn about His sufficient grace and His hands on our life.

Becoming God's masterpiece involves exchanging our emphasis on self-centeredness to being God-centered. It entails removing self from the throne of our lives and giving God His rightful place. Willingly submitting in a servant's attitude requires ultimate humility—total surrender.

To be totally surrendered requires that we put our life in the Potter's Hands. The Lord spoke to Jeremiah in these words: "Arise and go down to the potter's house, and there I will cause you to hear My words. Then I went down to the potter's house, and there he was, making something at the wheel. And the vessel that he made of clay was marred in the hand of the potter, so he made it again into another vessel, as it seemed good to the potter to make. Then the word of the Lord came to him, saying: 'O house of Israel, can I not do with you as this potter?' says the Lord. 'Look, as the clay is in the potter's hand, so are you in My hand, O house of Israel!'" (Jer. 18:1–6).

Several times in the Bible, reference is made to the analogy of God as the potter and us as clay. In Isaiah 64:8 (NLT), it says, "And yet, O Lord, you are our Father. We are the clay, and you are the potter. We all are formed by your hand." This analogy is one that the people in Isaiah's day could easily relate.

Have you ever watched anyone make pottery? Recently, I watched a demonstration of pottery being made as the potter's testimony was given with an analogy of the transformation that had occurred in her life through the molding and refining process. That process was beautiful as the potter transformed dull, wet clay into a beautiful piece of art. For the purpose of forming the clay, the potter had to have a perfectly balanced wheel while it was spun very quickly to shape the clay into the perfect pot.

As she demonstrated the process, we were challenged to personify our lives as the clay in the hands of the Potter. Just as clay, we are complex and mysterious, filled with impurities and can be difficult to mold. He places us on the wheel that spins very rapidly, and unless we are in the center, we typically get thrown off or are wobbly at best. Yet God is persistent with His love as He places his hands on the clay, putting the clay in the center of the wheel or His will, cupping His hands around our life to make sure it stays balanced. He smooths out our lumps and tests our pliability. No matter how many things seem to be spinning out of control, we need to stay in God's hands throughout the process. God never gives up.

After the Potter smooths out the edges and has us balanced, He does something interesting. He hollows out part of the clay as He does to us so that we can be filled with His love and purpose. He continues to reshape and remold us so we can grow into the likeness of Jesus. Finally, the Potter begins to shape the clay into the vessel of His choosing. He knew what He was going to make with a specific purpose in mind. If we were to view ourselves on the Potter's wheel, we might just see a lump of clay, but God sees us as an incredible work of art—a true masterpiece. In His omniscience, He looks at us, not as who we are, but who we will become. We are impatient and desire to have foresight of what is yet to come, but God works everything according to His will, in His time. His design is more than we could ever imagine. We just need to remember clay must be moldable if it is to be made into a useful vessel. Clay that is not moldable is not useful. Therefore, we, too, must stay in the Potter's Hands. John 15:4 must become a reality to us: "Abide in Me, and I in you. As the branch cannot bear fruit of itself unless it abides in the vine, so neither can you, unless you abide in Me." The person who abides in the Lord lives not for himself but for Christ.

Submission to God occurs only when He lives through us. His thoughts are our thoughts. His desires are our desires. We see through His eyes and experience courage when we are afraid, finding confidence in our times of uncertainty. Our focus must be aligned with a spiritual mind-set with a spiritual thirst for His Presence. It means "sitting before the Lord" in a time of stillness or meditation. Just as King David pursued this godly endeavor fervently and fruitfully, quietly waiting and reflecting on God, we, too, must seek after God's heart. David knew the significance of meditation as he saw his need for personal guidance during the times of turmoil he faced and so should we.

J. I. Packer describes a very inspirational meaning of meditation in his book *Knowing God*:

> Meditation is the activity of calling to mind, and thinking over, and dwelling on, and applying to oneself, the various things that one knows about the works and ways and purposes and promises of God. It is an activity of holy thought, cautiously performed in the presence of God, under the eye of God, by the help of God as a means of communion with God. Its purpose is to clear one's mental and spiritual vision of God and to let His truth make its full and proper impact on one's mind and heart. It is a matter of talking to oneself about God and oneself; it is, indeed, often a matter of arguing with oneself, reasoning oneself out of moods of doubt and unbelief into a clear apprehension of God's power and grace. Its effect is to ever humble us as we contemplate God's greatness and glory, and our littleness and sinfulness and to encourage and reassure us—"comfort" us in the old, strong Bible sense of the word—as we contemplate the unsearchable riches of divine mercy dis-

played in the Lord Jesus Christ. (*How*, Stanley, 94) (Packer)

Joshua 1:8 is a wonderful scripture on the blessed benefits of being still in the presence of our Lord. He said, "The Book of the Law shall not depart from your mouth, but you shall meditate in it all day and night, that you may observe to do according to all that is written in it. For then you will make your way prosperous, and then you will have good success."

Being still in meditation with the Lord is God's way of crowning our lives with His success and prosperity of soul, spirit, and body. It is also a catalyst to obedient living. Psalm 46:10 says, "Be still, and know that I am God." Meditation involves a dedicated time of commitment. It involves finding a place of solitude in which we focus on God and His holiness. In the book *How to Listen to God*, Charles Stanley stresses that meditation isn't a "spontaneous occurrence" but requires self-discipline if we are to reap the full benefits of a personal quiet time. Stanley expresses it this way: "We must take time for God. When/if we tell God we don't have time for Him, we are really saying we don't have time for life, for joy, for peace, for direction, or for prosperity, because He is the source of them all" (Stanley, 100).

Our time alone with God allows for praise and thanksgiving with an emphasis on listening and speaking to our Creator in sincerity and humility. It involves expressing our deepest thoughts, questions, and doubts. Yet if we simply want to be still and discern the presence of God in quiet, Psalm 62:5 urges us to "wait silently for God alone. For our expectation is from Him." We need to be sensitive to the power of God in our meditation and value His presence. Although the amount of time may be determined by a variety of factors, we must make it a priority, never giving the Lord our leftovers. The essence of meditation is a period set aside to fellowship with a holy God, in the throne room of His presence. As we enter His presence, we must prepare our minds and hearts in a repentant attitude to listen to Him and allow Him to permeate our spirits. Crucial to effective meditation is finding that place of solitude where we can be free from the distractions of the world around us as we open the windows to heaven. It is only then we can recognize God's benevolence, His omnipotence, and His grace. Through our stillness before the Lord, we can see His hand in everything occurring in our midst.

I wonder how many of us can identify with the following scenario:

> *All day long I had been very busy; picking up trash, cleaning bathrooms and scrubbing floors. My grown children were coming home for the weekend. I went grocery shopping and prepared for a barbecue supper, complete with ribs and chicken. I wanted everything to be perfect.*

> *Suddenly, it dawned on me that I was dog-tired. I simply couldn't work as long as I could when I was younger. "I've got to rest for a minute," I told my husband, Jim, as*

*I collapsed into my favorite rocking chair.
Music was playing, my dogs were chasing
each other, and the telephone rang.*

*A scripture from Psalm 46 popped into my
mind. "Be still, and know that I am God."
I realized that I hadn't spent much time in
prayer that day. Was I too busy to even utter
a simple word of thanks to God? Suddenly,
the thought of my beautiful patio came to
mind. I can be quiet out there, I thought.
I longed for a few minutes alone with God.*

*Jim and I had invested a great deal of time
and work in the patio that spring. The flowers and hanging baskets were breathtaking.
It was definitely a heavenly place of rest and
tranquility. If I can't be still with God in
that environment, I can't be still with Him
anywhere, I thought. While Jim was talking
on the telephone, I slipped out the backdoor
and sat down on my favorite patio chair. I
closed my eyes and began to pray, counting
my many blessings.*

*A bird flew by me, chirping and singing. It
interrupted my thoughts. It landed on the
bird feeder and began eating dinner as I
watched. After a few minutes, it flew away,
singing another song.*

I closed my eyes again. A gust of wind blew, which caused my wind chimes to dance. They made a joyful sound, but again I lost my concentration on God. I squirmed and wiggled in my chair. I looked up toward the blue sky and saw the clouds moving slowly toward the horizon. The wind died down. My wind chimes finally became quiet.

Again, I bowed in prayer. Honk, honk, *I heard. I almost jumped out of my skin. A neighbor was driving down the street. He waved at me and smiled. I waved back, happy that he cared. I quickly tried once again to settle down, repeating the familiar verse in my mind. "Be still and know that I am God."*

"I'm trying, God. I really am," I whispered. "But you've got to help me here."

The backdoor opened. My husband walked outside. "I love you," he said. "I was wondering where you were." I chuckled, as he came over and kissed me, then turned around and went back inside.

"Where's the quiet time?" I asked God. My heart fluttered. There was no pain, only a beat that interrupted me yet again. This

is impossible, I thought. There's no time to be still and to know that God is with me. There's too much going on in the world and entirely too much activity all around me.

Then it suddenly dawned on me. God was speaking to me the entire time I was attempting to be still. I remembered the music playing as I'd begun my quiet time. He sent a sparrow to lighten my life with song. He sent a gentle breeze. He sent a neighbor to let me know that I had a friend. He sent my sweetheart to offer sincere sentiments of love.

He caused my heart to flutter to remind me of life. While I was trying to count my blessings, God was busy multiplying them.

I laughed to realize that the "interruptions" of my quiet time with God were special blessings He'd sent to show me He was with me the entire time. (Gibbs)

After pondering this scenario, I readily identified with the many times in my life that have been characterized by moments that seemed so important in a worldly sense, yet in reality were unimportant in light of eternity. Too often God has spoken to me in His soft, sweet voice through the many unnoticed blessings He continually provides, even now. Father, help me to be sensitive to the precious moments in time when you speak—the beauty of your creative hands, the sounds of nature, and the kind, loving words of others.

"Although the world offers enticing substitutes, nothing can compare to the value of a genuine, growing, passionate relationship with Jesus. When our foremost passion is to know and experience God, we will spend time with Him. To hear His voice, we must be quiet and also remember that His presence 'doesn't always come to us when we are praying but also when we are not praying'" (Stanley, *Living*, 45, 46). We can experience Him through revelations that are signs of His handprint in everyday situations, whether it is in music, a sparrow, or expressions of love.

Our journey through life provides a multitude of experiences from our youth to our retirement. Yet, none of them can compare to what can be accomplished in the Artist's hands. We are in the process of becoming what God desires us to be—a portrait in the hands of God. Just as an artist selects various colors to squeeze, drip, or splatter his paint onto his canvas, the colors of our life are painstakingly painted on the canvas of our life to emulate the character of Jesus as we become more God-centered. It should be our ultimate desire that the character we portray will be one that is a reflection of His glory.

Both the artist and the potter are similar in their creative insights. The artist works with colors to depict an understanding of his subject, and the potter molds his pottery and paints it with a vision in mind. In both cases, it requires a process, one step at a time, one day at a time. In each design, there must be an element of trust that each will result in in a masterpiece of the creator.

Let us remain in the hands of our Creator.

Prayer

Dear Heavenly Father, we want to become the masterpiece You desire us to be. Although we see our lives as incomplete on the canvas of Your making, we know You see the final portrait. Help us to submit totally to You and allow You to paint the "colors of our life" in a way that brings You glory as we emulate the character of Jesus. Help us to put away our self-reliance and striving for worldly affirmation and look to You as the source of our wealth. As You hollow us out on the Potter's Wheel, may it be more of You and less of us. Please create in us a new heart and a true understanding of our position in Christ Jesus. Amen.

Victorious Over the Giants in Our Lives

*H*ave you ever met a giant? Not like the giant villains in fables and fairy tales, but those insurmountable problems or issues we face at one time or another in our lives. These giants are fearful foes that make us feel powerless and weak. Although we try to overcome them, they taunt us and seem only to grow stronger with the passing of time.

For some it may be the giant of experiences that remind us of events that caused fear that paralyzed us with our lack of confidence, creating discouragement, despair, and even depression. In a related way, a giant might be one of addiction, something that has a grip on our life. It may not even be drugs or alcohol but soap operas, media, or binge shopping. Then again, it could be a giant of greed or self-sufficiency that dominates some who name Christ as their Savior. Or it might be a different kind of giant altogether, like an unbelieving spouse or a prodigal child. Praying for them, we have asked the Lord to reach them. Yet they seem to become more hardened by apathy as the years pass by, causing us to question ourselves, "How can we overcome the burden it creates?"

How do we as Christians defeat the giants we face in our spiritual walk? How do we find the peace and joy that comes after being ambushed by such giants? We find the answer in the Old Testament account of David and Goliath (1 Sam. 17). What a victory! David boldly defeated the giant Goliath, armed only with a slingshot and five smooth stones.

There is so much we can learn from this story about being victorious in facing our giants in life. Let us examine at least five powerful stones we can use to defeat "our" giants:

- We all have giants that we come face-to-face with as we face hardships, obstacles, and temptations. Do you think David experienced any trepidation in his heart as he faced this towering giant? When we read the victory of David over Goliath, we see his determination, courage, and **faith**, the first stone he carried.

I have never faced a physical giant, but I have faced trials growing up as an only child seeking to understand about the family dynamics and assuming burdens far beyond my years. As I looked toward the future as a teenager, there were additional challenges as I pursued my bachelor's degree in education. There were times when I became ensnared by emotional giants of doubt, fear, disillusionment, insecurities, and uncertainty that tested my faith and testimony. The giants I faced didn't start out like Goliath as being 9 feet 6 inches tall. My giants often began quite small. Then, in time, they became bigger as I grew older and matured. My perceptions of things which I once accepted as the norm in early childhood became a disappointment and created despair when I realized the impact of alcohol within my home. Events that were intended for purposes of a joyous, spiritual celebration at Christmas became even bigger challenges in which I often wished would soon pass.

Although at times I felt what I experienced, no one else could understand. It was then I was reminded of 1 Corinthians 10:13 (NLT), "The temptations in your life are no different from what others experience. And God is faithful. He will not allow the temptation to be more than you can stand. When you are tempted, he will show you a way out so that you can endure." It was then that I realized my need for the power of the presence of God to carry me, molding me each step of the way. I truly believe that it was during those times that He began to fashion within me commitments and promises to Him which I try to hold true even today.

- Just as David, we have to understand that our modern-day Goliaths have some of the same challenges he faced. David knew of the faithfulness of God he had seen in the fields as a shepherd; therefore, he realized the need for his obedience as he received his call from God. We, too, must examine our conditions from a heavenly perspective. We can be a champion over the Goliaths in our life but must understand it requires a choice. "Our battles are

between God and the enemy of our souls—Satan."
Peer pressure and family influence often require
choices of a spiritual nature. Personally, although
difficult, I found for me to be victorious, I had to
be obedient to the promises I made to God during
the times of my need. **Obedience** was the second
stone David carried.

- David knew that faith and obedience alone would
  not allow victory against the Giant he faced. Victory
  could only come if he put his faith and obedience
  into action with the assurance that the battle was
  God's. "This is the Lord's battle, and he will give
  you to us!" (1 Sam. 17:47). David knew he had to
  put **action** to his faith, the third stone.

- When fighting against the giants in our life, we
  must call on God in prayer. Without prayer, we
  will be defeated. Of over the 7,487 promises in
  the Bible, I hold fast to the promise that "when
  believers pray, great things happen" (James 5:16,
  NCV). I have seen prayer transform the lives of
  people physically, socially, emotionally, and spiritually. I trust in the power of prayer and I know of
  a certainty that when I am faithful in prayer there
  is no obstacle I cannot face, especially if measured
  against the size of my God. Just as Paul expressed
  it, "I can do all things through Him who strength-
  ens me" (Phil. 4:13). The fourth stone David carried was **prayer** and one I embrace faithfully.

- In the witness of David as he went against Goliath, he not only had faith, was obedient, took action, and prayed, but he relied on the power of the Spirit of God to be with him. In any obstacle we face, we must face it with humility and reverence for God, recognizing our limitations and knowing the power in the God we serve. We must never measure the giants in our life by "our" strength. The fifth stone was found in the presence of the **Holy Spirit** for His empowerment.

Instead of using armor given to him by Saul, David knew from his experiences the faithfulness of His God. God was the source of his confidence. No matter the battle we face in life, we never go into combat alone or weaponless. The five smooth stones David carried in his shepherd's bag represent the faith, obedience, action, prayer, and gift of the Holy Spirit each of us carry when we face the Goliaths in our life.

David's confidence in God ultimately allowed a victory with one simple pebble to hit like a boulder against Goliath. We, too, are empowered to fight the giants in our life victoriously if we go into each conflict knowing all things are in the hands of God. He determines the outcome and will in the end be glorified (*Five Smooth Stones of: Faith, Obedience, Service, Prayer, and Holy Ghost*)

Prayer

Father, as we come into Your holy presence, help us be aware of the giants we face and the One who is responsible for their victory. Equip us to claim the confidence and assurance that helps us overcome, drawing our strength from You and Your promises.

FIGHTING OUR BATTLES
ON OUR KNEES

*I*n the first chapter, we began looking at becoming a masterpiece of God's design in the Potter's Hand. I used an analogy of a potter molding and making pottery through the process of taking a lump of clay and molding it into a vessel that He perceives it can become. As creations of our Father, it was my intention to paint a picture of us being in the center of the Potter's "wheel" or will as He places His hands around our life, emptying us of ourselves, making us into the vessel of His design. Our responsibility in that process rests in our total surrender—submitting our life to God and allowing Him to live His life through us.

Surrender is not easy for us because we are taught to be independent and self-sufficient, qualities considered admirable in a worthy character. Yet to be molded into the design of God's making, we must willingly allow Him to hollow us out on His potter's wheel, filling us with the desires of His heart above our own. To submit selflessly often requires an intimacy that comes as a result of experiencing a spiritual drought in times of our life which we find can only be satisfied by His holy presence.

In the eyes of the world, intimacy with our Father is classified as "religion," but intimacy is a relationship, a fellowship that is personal and a way of life. This personal intimacy involves communion with God to begin the day in prayer, praising Him in gratitude for the gift of life, and the blessings He continually showers upon us as we seek His leadership and guidance throughout the day. Starting our day in prayer should only be the beginning. Prayer should be continuous, whether we are lying down, sitting, walking, or kneeling.

Although I attended church as a child, I never understood what it truly meant to have a personal communion with God. I had heard others pray in church and at meals, but they seemed to be rote prayers rather than a personal conversation with God. As a child, I remember kneeling at the side of my bed, praying, "Now I lay me down to sleep. I pray the Lord my soul to keep. If I should die before I wake, I pray to God my soul to take. Amen."

I suppose this was a childhood beginning as I became aware of the need for reverence in prayer as I knelt in His presence. Over time that time of daily prayer ceased. Was it because I considered it a childlike habit that I had outgrown? Possibly so, but later I turned once again to God in prayer. As my parents began to drink habitually at night, weekends and holidays, I became lonely, depressed, and experienced a role reversal in which I had the need to protect them from what I felt other family and friends were unaware.

Recognizing the harm, it was causing to them physically and to me emotionally, I even found myself going to where the whiskey was hidden, getting it and pouring it out. If family came to visit, I would make excuses that my parents were sick and in bed. Not until much later did I realize that what I thought I had concealed was common knowledge.

In addition to the alcoholism, my father experienced multiple symptoms of mental illness and was committed repeatedly. Often, I was the only one that could persuade him of his need for help and would accompany him to the facility, telling him goodbye through locked doors.

I think each of us come to a time or place in our life when we face situations or circumstances that we cannot resolve alone. It is then we know there is One to whom we can carry our burdens through the power of prayer. "Come unto me, all [ye] that labour and are heavy laden, and I will give you rest" (Matt. 11:28, KJV).

The utter despair I felt goes beyond saying I needed unconditional love from God and His strength to hold me up when I felt I could not go on. It was during this time I began to pray more intently. Although there were times plagued by periods of loneliness, fear, and uncertainty, I still knew my parents loved me. Being raised in a middle-income family, my parents made sacrifices to provide our needs. My father worked in a factory, and my mother worked in a bank. There weren't many vacations or family trips, but I never considered what I was missing.

From the time I was born, there was no question if I would go to college. Neither of my parents had that opportunity. Therefore, the importance of an education for me took on greater meaning, especially for my father, who greatly desired one but never had that opportunity. No sacrifice was too great for him to make for it to be an inevitable privilege for me. I can even recall seeing my father wearing holes in the soles of his shoes to make it attainable. With college loans and parental sacrifices, it still would not have been possible without the kindness of an uncle who paid for a summer session. My parents had been taught the importance of unselfishness and instilled within me the value of thoughtfulness and appreciation for the generosity of others.

When I was a senior in high school and began thinking about leaving home for college, there was a vacuum within my heart that I knew had to be filled. It was then that I developed a personal relationship with God, characterized by the spiritual intimacy that I was in need of. It was then that I became totally transparent of my every need, every desire, and every request within my heart. For the first time I began to understand the richness of prayer. It wasn't just asking and receiving from God but a personal interaction, seeking to know His will for my life on my knees in a time of worship in His holy presence.

When I left for college, my need for His presence continued as I faced concerns of which I had no control—concern for my parents with their addiction and all the insecurities of being faced with new challenges away at college. Yet I knew the greatest place to face and fight my battles was on my knees. In His strength, I would find victory in the battlefield of my life.

To this day, I know God always answers prayers. There are requests we lift up to God that would seemingly bring Him glory, but they are not readily answered. Healing of a friend or loved one, physically or spiritually? family challenges? return of a prodigal son? I so often question God, why? Yet through the years, I have witnessed that there are reasons for the delays in answered prayers. The delays may be purpose-driven as He desires to seek our degree of persistence.

Interestingly, too often prayer is our last resource. We seek all the help resources that line the shelves of our book stores and other human resources before bowing before our almighty God for His wisdom and discernment. Our prayer to God should never be our last resort but our first step and should exemplify our commitment to prayer until the answer comes. Have you ever noticed how inconsistent our prayer life is? We offer momentary prayers today but forget to pray tomorrow, never bringing those prayers up again. All of us experience multiple distractions when we strive to devote ourselves to consecrated prayer and the cause of those distractions is Satan, our greatest adversary. Satan has no defense if we pray persistently, without ceasing. This will be a confession to others that we will seek what we need from the hand of God—the source of our every need. We must pray faithfully as we wait on His answer. Prayers aren't always answered as quickly as we desire, but one thing is certain, His timing is always perfect. If we will pray as Jesus did, "Not our will but thy will be done," we can be assured of an answer. We have a power in our prayer life that releases spiritual resources within us for His divine power and protection regardless of our circumstances or satanic attacks we face. In Ephesians 6:18, Paul wrote, "With all prayer and petition, pray at all times in the Spirit." The combat zone in which we live each day allows us to face it in the armor of prayer and sufficiency of our omnipotent Father. He knows our innermost parts, the inner recesses of our hearts, even our unspoken words but still seeks communion with us as we seek His grace.

Have you ever wondered what God sees when He examines our heart? Does our communion with Him reflect genuine unselfishness characterized by humility and brokenness with a desire to glorify Him, or does He see a heart with our self-centered motives seeking to bring us vain glory?

There have been prayer requests which have been persistently offered, and the answers came within days, weeks, some in months, others longer, but some yet to be answered, but I still wait with positive expectation. I believe that those on which I wait will be granted but only in God's time, only when I am in the spiritual position to receive them. They will be wrapped in His glory and will touch not only my life, but the others they have the opportunity to influence. When we glorify God rather than bring glory to ourselves, God will listen and answer. "Whatsoever ye shall ask in my name, that will I do, that the Father may be glorified in the Son" (John 14:13). "With all prayer and petition, pray at all times in the Spirit" (Eph. 6:18). "For God, who commanded the light to shine out of darkness, hath shined in our hearts, to give the light of the knowledge of the glory of God in the face of Jesus Christ" (2 Cor. 4:6, KJV).

When we lift our voices up to heaven in fervent prayer, we must remember God will not work through our eloquent, intellectual words or higher educational endeavors to obtain things for our selfish motives and comforts in life. God knows what we need before we ask Him. When we pray and ultimately seek answers to our prayers, they must be aligned with the heart of God to bring glory to the work He seeks to achieve through us. When we come before our Father in prayer, we must come with a passion of humility and sincerity openly conveying the transparency of our heart in communication to our Holy God. It does not require a specific formula for a prayer to be heard nor does it require a specific stance.

Throughout scripture, a variety of positions (bowing, standing, sitting, walking, lying prostrate, and kneeling) were used to demonstrate the attitudes of those praying. Since prayer for each of us is very personal, our only required prerequisite is a repentant heart of reverence with the desire for a personal fellowship with our Father. Often, in "our" trials, we recognize our need to pray for strength, wisdom, or discernment, recognizing our weaknesses and insufficiency. But there are also times when God through the power of the Holy Spirit speaks to us, urging and convicting us to come into His holy presence that we might experience peace that only He can provide.

There have been multiple times when God has come to me, spoken, and urged me to fight specific battles on my knees. During those times, He has come to me with a power of which I had never experienced previously.

On one particular occasion at a time when I was extremely worried about a family member who was experiencing extreme depression and hopelessness, I had such an encounter. In the midst of a deep sleep, God came to me and spoke. His Presence was so strong that I was awakened and sat up in the middle of my bed to listen. Although my husband, who was asleep beside me, was not awakened, I heard the voice clearly. He told me to get up and go to the living room, kneel on my knees, and pray. I immediately responded as directed. As I kneeled on my knees in that room, I knew I was in the presence of God in a holy place. I was assured, "Do not be anxious about anything, but in every situation, by prayer and petition, with thanksgiving, present your requests to God. And the peace of God, which transcends all understanding, will guard your hearts and your minds in Christ Jesus" (Phil. 4:6–7, NIV). That night as I got off my knees, I knew with confidence my worry and the feelings of my desperation were in His hands.

Could it be that as we wait on our unanswered prayers, God is testing our faith? There were many biblical patriarchs whose faith was tested beyond our imagination. Yet their faith allowed them to witness God's unshakable promises that led them into a closer walk in His presence.

- There was Job who faced trials of suffering physically, emotionally, and spiritually, but his love never wavered. He remained steadfast in his faithfulness. "In all this Job did not sin or charge God with wrong." (Job 1:22)
- Noah was a man given a task that would appear to us insurmountable. He was to build an ark for himself, and his family as well as two of each kind, male and female, of all animals and birds,

36

along with food for all of them. At God's command Noah listened without reluctance and acted. "Noah did this; he did all that God commanded him." (Gen. 6:22)

- Abraham was a hundred years old when he and Sarah were blessed with Isaac in their old age. At the age of about ten years old, Isaac was to be offered as a sacrifice under the direction of God. As a parent, I cannot imagine the thoughts that must have gone through Abraham's mind as he walked slowly to the top of Mount Moriah with Isaac. However, Abraham's faith in the promises of God was once again confirmed. "And the angel of the Lord called unto him out of heaven, and said, Abraham, Abraham: and he said, Here am I. And he said, lay not thine hand upon the lad, neither do thou anything unto him; for now I know that thou fearest God, seeing thou hast not withheld thy son, thine only son from me." (Gen. 22:11–12, KJV)

- Our perfect role model of faith in the power of prayer is Jesus. It was Jesus who taught the disciples to pray and found strength in fellowship with His Father when He fought his most arduous battles. Two specific occasions that come to mind are the times when Jesus was in the Garden of Gethsemane and as He was being crucified. In the garden, he faced the horror and agony of what was ahead. Falling on his knees, Jesus asked to be spared if it was possible. "My soul is overwhelmed with sorrow to the point of death. He fell with his face to the ground and prayed, my Father, if it is possible, may this cup be taken from me. Yet, not as I will, but as you will." (Matt. 22:38–39)

The other defining moment was when Jesus hung on the cross. Following the beatings, flogging, and the pain from the piercing of the thorns in His head, we were still on His mind. Although it was our sins that nailed him there, Jesus said, 'Father, forgive them, for they do not know what they are doing" (Luke 23:34).

In these examples, acts of faith resulted in a closer walk with God. Do you ever wonder how God would classify our faith if we were confronted with the same commands?

If we had experienced the death of each member in our family as Job, not to mention the other trials of testing he faced, would we have praised God or hurled insults at him?

If we had been assigned to build an ark and have to focus on the challenges that would lie ahead—the utter destruction and punishment of mankind; listening to those wailing for entrance into the ark as they gasped for their last breath, would we have listened and been obedient or ignored the command with disbelief?

If we had been childless for a hundred years as Abraham, would we have trusted God for a substitutional sacrifice or fled in unadulterated fear?

If we had been in the Garden of Gethsemane experiencing the anguish of the cross to the point of sweating blood, would we have fled from the garden seeking a means of escape?

If it had been us in the garden arrested by the soldiers, followed by the beatings, flogging, and cursing, would we have shown the same compassion as Jesus on the cross, or would we have blasphemed God?

Although we might be unsure of our responses, these spiritual patriarchs were obedient because they knew of the faithfulness of God. Regardless of the encounters they faced, they trusted in the power of God for His wisdom, discernment, and strength. It is in these acts of trust that our resolve is tested as we stand firm in the One who gives us life. Paul reminds us that we should "stand firm. Let nothing move you. Always give yourselves fully to the work of the Lord, because you know that your labor in the Lord is not in vain" (1 Cor. 15:58).

Just as these men's faith was founded on their relationship with God, we, too, will find our fellowship with God through prayer on our knees is the source of all our victory.

Yet recently, I have questioned the degree to which "my" faith impacts my prayer life. How strong is my faith? Is it little or great in the eyes of God? How is it measured in comparison with the mustard seed? In Matthew 17:20, Jesus said, "Because of the littleness of your faith; for truly I say to you, if you have faith the size of a mustard seed; you will say to this mountain, 'Move from here to there,' and it will move; and nothing will be impossible to you."

There are prayers I offer to God while lying down, on my daily walks, sitting, and kneeling. Some prayers have been answered. Others are yet to be. Do I have mustard seed faith for the answers that are yet to come? Jesus speaks figuratively when He speaks of the mustard seed to illustrate that little is much when it comes to God. His power is incalculable when He unleashes it in our lives. It is through our faith, as tiny as a mustard seed, that will bring glory to God and influence those within our influence.

Lifting our prayers up to our Father must be based on faith—not questioning if God will answer but listening and watching for how He will answer. Even those prayers on which we wait will be answered in His divine timing.

As we strive to become the masterpiece that God has chosen us to be, we must face every battle on our knees in prayer, trusting in His divine power, protection, and faithfulness. Let us faithfully commune with our Father in prayer, listening obediently to Him. He has great and mighty things in store for each of us.

A young man had been to Wednesday night Bible study. The pastor had spoken about "listening to God and obeying the Lord's voice."

The young man couldn't help but wonder, "Does God still speak to people?"

After service, he went out with some friends for coffee and pie, and they discussed the message. Several different ones talked about how God had led them in different ways. It was about ten o'clock when the young man started driving home. Sitting in his car, he just began to pray, "God, if you still speak to people, speak to me. I will listen. I will do my best to obey."

As he drove down the main street of his town, he had the strangest thought to stop and buy a gallon of milk. He shook his head and said out loud, "God, is that you?" He didn't get a reply, so he started on toward home. But again, the thought came to him: buy a gallon of milk.

The young man thought about Samuel, and how he didn't recognize the voice of God, and how little Samuel ran to Eli. "Okay, God, in case that is you, I will buy the milk."

It didn't seem like too hard a test of obedience. He could always use the milk. So he stopped and purchased the gallon of milk and started toward home.

As he passed Seventh Street, he again felt the urge, "Turn down that street." This is crazy, he thought, and drove on past the intersection. Again, he felt that he should turn down Seventh Street. At the next intersection, he turned back and headed down Seventh.

*Half jokingly, he said out loud, "Okay, God,
I will."*

*He drove several blocks, when suddenly, he
felt like he should stop. He pulled over to
the curb and looked around. He was in a
semi-commercial area of town. It wasn't the
best, but it wasn't the worst of neighborhoods
either. The businesses were closed, and most
of the houses looked dark, like people were
already in bed.*

*Again, he sensed something, "Go and give
the milk to the people in the house across the
street."*

*The young man looked at the house. It was
dark and it looked like the people were either
gone or they were already asleep. He started
to open the door and then sat back in the car
seat. "Lord, this is insane. Those people are
asleep, and if I wake them up, they are going
to be mad and I will look stupid."*

*Again, he felt like he should go and give the
milk. Finally, he opened the door and said,
"Okay, God, if this is you, I will go to the
door and I will give them the milk. If you
want me to look like a crazy person, okay. I
want to be obedient. I guess that will count*

for something but, if they don't answer right away, I am out of here."

He walked across the street and rang the bell. He could hear some noise inside. A man's voice yelled out, "Who is it? What do you want?"

Then the door opened before the young man could get away. The man was standing there in his jeans and T-shirt. He looked like he just got out of bed. He had a strange look on his face, and he didn't seem too happy to have some stranger standing on his doorstep.

The man asked, "What is it?"

The young man thrust out the gallon of milk and said, "Here, I brought this to you," he said.

The man took the milk and rushed down a hallway speaking loudly in Spanish. Then from down the hall came a woman carrying the milk toward the kitchen. The man was following her holding a baby. The baby was crying. The man had tears streaming down his face.

The man began speaking and half crying, "We were just praying. We had some big bills this month and we ran out of money. We didn't have any milk for our baby. I was just praying and asking God to show me how to get some milk."

His wife in the kitchen yelled out, "I ask him to send an angel with some. Are you an Angel?"

The young man reached into his wallet and pulled out all the money he had on him and put it in the man's hand. Then he turned and walked back toward his car and tears were streaming down his face. He knew then that God does still speak to people...and answer prayers. (Gospelweb.net)

When our prayers are answered during our time of personal need, does God send angels unaware to us? Does He speak to others in ways that even they don't understand but respond because of that sweet small voice that urges them to respond? As we pray in a spirit of urgency, characterized by the humility of a broken spirit such as a mother who needs milk for a crying baby, we are reminded that we must remember that He is "able to do immeasurably more than all we ask or imagine" (Eph. 3:20).

Our Heavenly Father knows each and every encounter we face. He knows where we are on the battlefield in our life's journey and the degree to which our faith wavers.

Let us never fail to remember that even during our times of weakness, we have a great intercessor that prays on our behalf.

> When we forget to pray, he remembers to
> pray.
> When we are full of doubt, he is full of
> faith.
> When we are unworthy to be heard, he
> is ever worthy to be heard. (Lucado,
> *Unshakable* 86)

Prayer is the doorway to the heart of God. If we are to strive to become God's masterpiece, we must realize that we will face obstacles along the way that may cause us to trip in foxholes, but let us also remember we cannot stumble when we are on our knees. There is no better place to find victory than on our knees.

Prayer

Our Father, help us to come into Your presence, bowing on our knees, before Your throne of grace. Help us to know and understand that we are truly in the process of becoming the masterpiece of Your design. In that process of becoming, help us to relinquish every battle we face into Your care. Thank you for the power of prayer.

BEING ALERT TO HIS VOICE

*W*hen we reflect on the many times Jesus prayed, we recognize that He knew the power of being in the presence of His Father. Jesus found strength, peace, power, and rest as He came into the solitude of God's presence. Not only did He lift up His voice to heaven, He knew that to fulfill the purpose for which He was called, it required an attitude of humility and reverence. In the stillness of those moments, He tuned His ear to listen for the voice of His Father for His divine wisdom and discernment in preparation for the hours, days, and weeks ahead.

What was the spiritual atmosphere Jesus desired through His expression of submission to God's authority as He prayed? To become the masterpiece of His creation, we must seek a place of personal, private meditation in which we not only speak but learn to listen. Jesus prayed in a number of different places to include the desert, on the mountain, at the temple, and in the Garden of Gethsemane. Each setting was a place in which His communion with God would be set apart from the rush, noise, and distractions of the world. His ultimate goal was one that each of us should desire—to be lost in the peace and presence of our Creator.

To be alert to our Master's voice, we must know the importance of prayer and understand our communion with

Him is not a monologue, a one-way conversation. Instead, it is a majestic experience in which we learn how to listen. In Proverbs 8:34, Solomon exclaims, "Blessed is the man who listens to me, watching daily at my gates, waiting at the posts of my doors."

Have our lives become so complex and preoccupied with the distractions of the world that we have "drifted out of the listening range" of God when He speaks? To hear Him when He speaks, we must seek perfect communion through intentional solitude with our Heavenly Father. Only then can we experience the resilience and decisiveness that transcends our circumstances.

When God speaks to us, He speaks with precious treasures He chooses to reveal to us. Through the power of the Holy Spirit, we are given the spiritual understanding for His truth as clarified through the words of Paul in 1 Corinthians 2:9–10, "Eye has not seen, nor ear heard, nor have entered into the heart of man the things which God has prepared for those who love Him. But God has revealed them through His Spirit. For the Spirit searches all things, yes, the deep things of God." The revelations of God's treasures equip us with a deeper understanding of who He is—His holiness, His power, and His majesty. He makes known His eternal plans for each of us as He molds us into His likeness. God's abiding presence within us through the Holy Spirit make available to us all of His spiritual resources, including access to His wisdom and righteousness. "God made him who had no sin to be sin for us, so that in him we might become the righteousness of God" (2 Cor. 5:21, NIV).

Another treasure He affords us is seeing others through His spiritual eyes. As we commune with God in prayer, we witness the transformative power of a changed heart with new eyes. Our heart becomes tender, and we see through His eyes of love rather than judgment. Through His eyes of love, we recognize that each of His creations have been designed with a divine purpose in mind.

With God's divine purpose in mind for each of us, He seeks to communicate with us his infinite love and definite direction for our lives through wise and spiritual counsel. For every need, sorrow, and uncertainty, He provides words of comfort and assurance.

The greatest treasure God provides through His communication with us is the intimacy to know Him better. Whenever we desire to establish personal relationships with others, it requires that we have open conversations based on trust and transparency. The same is true with God. He wants us to have conversation with Him, conveying our innermost concerns but also listening to Him as He speaks.

If you ask a broad range of the population today if they believe God still speaks today, you would get a variety of responses. Some would respond with a resounding "No." Others might respond that God only spoke in the Bible through dreams, prophets, or angels. Yet others, even some Christians, might think it is possible but not certain.

For biblical scholars and people who are students of the Word, their answers would be based on personal affirmation and experience. Having been a follower of Christ for over fifty years, I have heard God speak to me through scripture, through the Holy Spirit, through circumstances, and godly people.

Through God's revelation to me in my study of scripture, I believe the Bible is the inerrant, inspired Word of God that is God-breathed on those who wrote it. It reveals the truth of God by God. As God speaks to me in His Word, He shows me the foundation of my faith through His love and sacrifice with a model for everyday living.

God also speaks through the power of the Holy Spirit who indwells us. Seemingly, not all people recognize or understand the role of the Holy Spirit within our lives. There is one God, and the Holy Spirit is one of the Trinity who was promised to come as our Helper and Comforter when Jesus joined God in heaven. When He came at Pentecost, we were blessed with His presence to reveal a deeper understanding of the reality of God and the cost of our salvation through His death and resurrection. The Holy Spirit speaks to us with His wisdom for the interpretation of scripture. "Then He opened their minds, so they could understand the scriptures. He told them, 'This is what is written: The Messiah will suffer and rise from the dead on the third day, and repentance for the forgiveness of sins will be preached in His name to all nations, beginning at Jerusalem'" (Luke 24:45–47, NIV).

The Holy Spirit speaks to us as He brings the convicting power of God for the realization of our need for a Savior. It is He who makes our heart pliable to hear and act on the condition of our heart for repentance and salvation. He not only speaks to us but also speaks as an intercessor for us before God, our Father. The Holy Spirit speaks and prays for us when we do not know how to pray as we should. He lifts up our every need in the throne room of God in the presence of our omnipotent Father.

Through reflections in my life, I know God speaks in our circumstances. Experiences in our life can reveal many emotions. Some are joyous, while others invoke anger, disappointments, or sadness, but God has spoken to me through all of these and far more. In each circumstance, He has taught me lessons of thankfulness, humility, and patience. At the times when I faced these events, I was unaware of the messages God was seeking to reveal to me. In each moment when I felt things were falling apart or I felt I was all alone or that I couldn't go on, I heard that sweet, quiet voice that reminded me that He was in the midst of every situation with His presence and strength to hold me up. The Holy Spirit reminded me of the words in Romans 8:28, "And we know that in all things God works for the good of those who love Him, who have been called according to His purpose." I learned a very valuable lesson as He spoke. In each situation, it doesn't mean that the circumstances need to change. Instead, it is me who needs to change as I learn to rely on the One who is my hope and strength.

God has blessed me with people in my life that have taught me through their spiritual example and words of wisdom. In most cases, they were unaware of the impact their witness had on me. If I am perfectly honest, I must admit I did not recognize their influence until they died, but in retrospect, I know now they left a legacy on my life that has had an eternal impact. They include Sunday school teachers that proclaimed the Word of God unashamedly, my grandmother who read God's word faithfully and attended church regularly, and an aunt that taught the Bible every Sunday, as well as, play the piano in church.

I know that in God's eternal purpose, He has orchestrated each of these godly people, then and now, to speak to me about His love and message. There are people today who God uses to speak to me through their godly example as their life exemplifies the hands, feet, and mouth of Jesus.

Each of these people who I have encountered throughout my life through God's divine plan has altered the course of my life through their example, encouraging words or opportunities they have afforded to me. Each of them has and will continue to be instruments of His handiwork in my life. It is the desire of my heart that just as all of these have impacted my spiritual walk, I can pass it on to others—those I love and care about.

God does speak to us through godly people. We never know to what degree our influence or God's words through us can transform the lives of others. Could it be that God has a message He has chosen for us to deliver?

Regardless of how God speaks to us or what it takes to get our attention, He does speak. When God speaks everyone should listen, and we should demonstrate the wisdom of David when he declared in Psalm 85:8, "I will listen to what God the Lord will speak."

Yet will we listen? Or will we have selective hearing?

In the parable of the sower in Matthew 13:1–23, we are reminded of the many **barriers** we experience when God speaks. The seed in the parable is the gospel message of God, and the soil represents the condition of the human heart.

- One of the barriers to hearing God is a **heart hardened by the sin** in our life that leads us to the rejection of the truth of God as we rebel due to personal arrogance.

- The second barrier to hearing the voice of God is when His Word fails to take root in our heart due to **"rocky" circumstances of trouble or persecution** that challenge our faith. There are times when we do not immediately see the hand of God in our trials, but we can always trust His heart.

- A third barrier that "chokes" or tunes us out from the voice of God consists of the **thorns of desires** for acquisition of more things and greater wealth. To avoid such a hindrance, we must trust God to deliver us from worries, and the deceitfulness of wealth that prevent us from hearing God.

- In contrast to the first three barriers, we see good soil in which God's word is heard and believed through an open heart. When we recognize our heart has become hardened and characterized by rocky circumstances and choked by the thorns of worldly possessions, we can allow the divine Gardener to transform the condition of our hearts that we will be sensitive to His voice and hear Him when He speaks.

I believe that each of us have experienced periods of spiritual drought in our life when we have allowed hindrances to prevent us from listening to the voice of God. There may have also been moments in which we have felt the convicting power of the Holy Spirit to listen to His voice with an urgency to respond and then dismissed it.

From the experiences in my life, I must honestly admit, I have been insensitive to the voice of God due to turning a deaf ear to what He wanted to say. During some of those times, there appeared to be no detrimental outcomes, but at other times, I know listening became a matter of eternal consequence.

Is there something He is trying to say to us? Are we truly listening? Could it be that what He is saying doesn't just affect us?

His name was Bill. He had wild hair, wore a T-shirt with holes in it, jeans, and no shoes. This was literally his wardrobe for his entire four years of college. He was brilliant. Kind of esoteric and very, very bright. He had become a Christian recently while attending college.

Across the street from the campus was a well-dressed, very conservative church. One day Bill decided to go there. He walked in with no shoes, jeans, his T-shirt, and wild hair. The service had already started, so Bill started down the aisle to look for a seat.

The church was completely packed, and he couldn't find a seat. By now people were really looking a bit uncomfortable, but no one said anything. Bill got closer and closer and closer to the pulpit, and when he realized there were no seats, he just squatted down right on the carpet. (Although perfectly acceptable behavior at a college fellowship, trust me, this had never happened in this church before!)

By now the people were really uptight, and the tension in the air was thick. About this time, the minister realized that from way at the back of the church, a deacon was slowly making his way toward Bill. The deacon was in his eighties, had silver-gray hair, and a three-piece suit. A godly man, very elegant, very dignified, very courtly. He walked with a cane and, as he started walking toward this boy, everyone began saying to themselves, "You can't blame him for what he's going to do. How can you expect a man of his age and of his background to understand some college kid on the floor?"

It took a long time for the man to reach the boy. The church was utterly silent except for the clicking of the man's cane.

All eyes were focused on him. You couldn't even hear anyone breathing. The minister couldn't even preach the sermon until the deacon did what he had to do. They saw this elderly man drop his cane on the floor. With great difficulty, he lowered himself and sat down next to Bill and worshiped with him so he wouldn't be alone.

Everyone choked up with emotion. When the minister gained control, he said, "What I'm about to preach, you will never remember. What you have just seen, you will never forget." (Inspirational Christian Connection)

Is it possible the deacon heard the sweet, soft voice of God speak? When God speaks, we never know the outcome or the hearts that will be touched if we will only listen. Our time on earth is precious and quickly fleeting. How will we spend it? "Every waking moment we communicate a message whether it is by what we say or fail to say, by what we do or fail to do" (Stanley, *How*, 28).

We are in the process of becoming a masterpiece in the Potter's Hands. God knows our life is not yet what we will be when we step into His eternal presence but until that time, He is shaping our life, conforming us into the image of His Son. It is through His grace that this transformation is possible.

Prayer

Father, as we set ourselves apart for the time of solitude that allows us to spend time with You, help us to be alert to Your words and apply them to our every need. Let us not be distracted by those things around us that prevent us from sensing Your holy presence and discerning Your will for our lives.

EMPOWERMENT BY THE HOLY SPIRIT
"NOTHING GREATER THAN HIS PRESENCE"

*I*n the book *Just Give Me Jesus*, there is a story told by Anne Graham Lotz:

> *A man who walked into a hardware store and told the clerk that due to an enormous storm the previous night, a large oak tree had crashed into his yard.*
>
> *Although the tree had not hit his house, the main trunk was lying across his driveway, and the huge branches were crisscrossing the front lawn and blocking his view. So he was interested in buying the very best chainsaw that the clerk had to sell.*
>
> *The clerk, who had listened sympathetically to the man's tale of woe, nodded and said he had just the thing. He excused himself for a moment, disappeared into the back stockroom, then reemerged, carrying a huge Stihl*

chainsaw encased in an orange plastic housing. The clerk described the features of the saw, but when he said it could cut through the giant oak tree like a knife through soft butter, the man needed no further sales pitch. He opened his wallet, paid for the saw, and lugged it out of the store.

Three days later the man came back into the hardware store, dragging the big chain saw. His hair was disheveled, his face was covered in a bristly three-day-old beard, his clothes were sweaty, dirty, and smelly, and his face was scrunched into an angry scowl. He dropped the saw on the floor. Then he smacked the counter with his fist and in a hoarse, raspy voice, began to yell at the clerk, "I thought you said this was the best saw you had for sale! I thought you said this saw was so good and fast, it would cut through the oak tree like a knife through butter. Well. I've been sawing for three full days, and I've only gotten through two tiny limbs. I want my money back because this saw doesn't work!"

As other customers stopped and stared, the clerk, who had been standing in shocked amazement at the sudden outburst, moved swiftly to exercise damage control. As he quickly walked around the counter, he *responded defensively, "That saw was in perfect working order when I sold it to you." He then reached down to the saw and pulled its little black cord. Immediately, the saw sprang to life with a loud roar. The man jerked upright, his eyes wide with astonishment as he exclaimed, "What's that noise?"*

The poor man had been trying to use a chainsaw to cut wood without ever activating the power! (Lotz, 152)

This story reminds me of many Christians who try living the Christian life without activating the power. The power to whom I refer is the Holy Spirit, the third Person of the Trinity and probably the least understood member of the Godhead. God the Father and Jesus His Son are familiar to most people, but when speaking of the Holy Spirit, He is referred to as an ethereal or celestial being. The reference most often made is during baptisms, benedictions, or associated with those with charismatic gifts but the Holy Spirit is not only for special occasions or select groups. The Holy Spirit is a person Who is imparted to every believer when we experience our conversion/transformation with a newness of life through Jesus.

Have there been times when you envied those who saw Jesus in the flesh, who walked with Him, talked to Him, and even touched Him? Have there been times when in the midst of a personal crisis, you have thought, "If only

I could hear His voice right now or just touch the hem of His garment!"

A couple of years ago during my devotional time, I began to yearn for a deeper, more intimate relationship with Jesus. I knew that it would require an understanding of the Holy Spirit, His power and purpose for my life. In my seventy-one years, I have heard very little preached or taught about the Holy Spirit and His power in our life. Due to the little knowledge I had of Him, I began to study scripture and seek God's wisdom for His understanding. Just as the disciples wanted to comprehend more fully the reason for Jesus's death, so did I. How did the death of Jesus impact the influence of the Holy Spirit? Examining the promises of God, He brought clarity to the revelation of the Holy Spirit, His purposes, and His ways.

When Jesus was about to go to His Father, He promised He would send the Holy Spirit to live within us. Speaking to the disciples, Jesus said, "But very truly I tell you, it is for your good that I am going away. Unless I go away, the Advocate [Holy Spirit] will not come to you, but if I go I will send Him to you" (John 16:7, NIV).

How could there be more benefit to having the Holy Spirit than the physical presence of Jesus? As I searched for the answers, I found there is so much more!

While Jesus was in the flesh, He was subject to the fleshly limitations of time and space. When Jesus stepped off His throne to take on earthly flesh, He humbled himself to make many sacrifices. Prior to coming to us, He was a Spirit, like God the Father and the Holy Spirit. He was omnipresent without the limitations of time or space. He dwelled everywhere in every point in time. As a sacrifice for us, He gave up His very existence of his nature that we might walk with and know the presence of God. Yet due to this sacrifice, only those who managed to get within an arm's reach could touch Him; only a few thousand at most could be within the sound of His voice. We are told in His Last Supper with His apostles that there was something better yet to come, His presence in the form of the Holy Spirit. In the era following His resurrection, Jesus told us He would not only be with us but also in us. "But you shall receive power when the Holy Spirit has come upon you; and you shall be my witnesses in Jerusalem and in all Judea and Samaria and to the end of the earth" (Acts 1:8).

As I began to understand the Person of the Holy Spirit, I came to know His purpose in me. I saw His personality as the transparency of Jesus shining through with His emotions (joy, comfort, grief, and conviction) and spiritual resources (instruction, intercession, strength, encouragement, and power) from which I could draw—all of which should glorify Him.

Each of us encounter despair, but in those periods of embarrassment, despondency, loneliness, or sadness, the Holy Spirit abides within us to show us that "joy comes in the morning" (Ps. 30:5). We have His assurance that the power of His might will replace those clouds with a silver lining of peace and comfort. "The LORD is my light and my salvation—whom shall I fear? The LORD is the stronghold of my life—of whom shall I be afraid?" (Ps. 27:1).

Are there moments in your life when you have experienced inner stirrings within you to say or do something, yet question its validity? I certainly have on more than one occasion.

One of the attributes I became strongly aware of was the convicting power of the Holy Spirit and the lessons I could learn. Oh! How He wants to speak to us and through us with the cry of his heart. If we will only pause, be still, and be sensitive to Who is speaking. The Holy Spirit speaks in a still small voice within us, often creating a concern, urging us to act, say something, or even directing us to speak His truth as we are used in touching others.

Several years ago, I went to our church office for a particular purpose and upon entering I sat by a lady who appeared to be very distraught, waiting to see a pastor. She was called back to the pastor's office without the opportunity to even introduce myself. On my way home, I got a strong concern within my heart to reach out to her. Not knowing her name, address, or telephone number, I called the church and told the pastor that the Lord had told me I had to go see her, requesting information that would allow me to visit.

I immediately followed up by going to see her. I told her that God had sent me to her and I would like to visit. While there, I found out she had been distraught with the recent loss of her son and had not only once but several times had attempted suicide. Having experi-

enced my father's suicide, I realized the urging of the Holy Spirit was the reason I was called upon to make this visit. God sent me there to be a friend and demonstrate God's love. Before leaving we prayed together. As I stood at the door to leave, I told her I loved her. She responded that she didn't know how to express her love and I told her that all she needed to know was that I loved her and God loves her even more.

Since that visit, I have spent precious time with her, assisting her around her home, praying with her and allowing God to use me as He leads. I am assured that the events of that day were orchestrated by the power of the Holy Spirit and His voice to me. I recognize that when He speaks, I must listen and obey.

The Holy Spirit does speak to me and has spoken to me many times in many ways, but I must admit I have not always listened. I am always reminded that to listen is a choice I make, and He will not violate my free will.

Have you ever felt the presence of the Holy Spirit speak as He urged you to respond in some way? He may have impressed on you the need to take some action or pray. Due to the timing or lack of your sensitivity to His voice, you failed to do so. Realizing later, had you done so, events might have been different, possibly resulting in eternal consequences.

God provides encounters that the Holy Spirit can bless if we are only available and willing to be used as an instrument to glorify Him. Yet He never violates our free will, instead, waits to determine if we will be sensitive to His voice and act in obedience. Our willingness to respond to the empowerment of the Holy Spirit is a reflection of our faith. "And without faith, it is impossible to please God because anyone who comes to him must believe he exists and that he rewards those who earnestly seek Him" (Heb. 11:6).

Faith is a gift from God (Eph. 2:8–9). However, there are times that the Holy Spirit reveals to us that the condition of our faith wavers. Just as Christ told his disciples that with just a tiny measure of it, the size of a mustard seed, they could move mountains. There are mountains all of us face as we walk in our journey of life. Some come in the forms of depression, illness, strained relationships, and other challenges. Yet I found that true faith brings victory through the power of the Holy Spirit. "You, dear children, are from God and have overcome them because the One who is in you is greater than the one who is in the world" (2 John 4:4, NIV).

In my life, I have had several mountains that had to be moved. Some greater than others but each one challenged my faith. Having come from a family that seemingly was plagued with periods of depression with multiple sui-

cides, I experienced first-hand the depths of despair resulting from the death of my father and facing postpartum depression myself after child birth.

The mountains of depression are real and can reach elevations that cannot be explained or even justified in the victims of those experiencing them. Even as a Christian, the depth of my valley experience made the mountain I faced seem insurmountable. The darkness that engulfed me was so overwhelming that even the love of God and the love of family could not deliver me from the pit in which I fell. In the midst of the darkness that overcame me, there was something (Someone) within me that told me to pray. Being alone with my two sons due to my husband's travel out of town, I had no interruptions, so I prayed! I prayed all night long with serious concern that unless there was intervention from God, I would not see the light of another day. I was to return to my teaching position the next day, a day at this point I was unsure would ever come.

Rather than being lifted from the depths of my despair, it worsened. I continued to pray to the One who had been faithful so many times in the past, but throughout the night

I could not find the hope I sought. The next day I reported to my position at school, bathing myself in prayer, on the verge of tears and a complete breakdown. Words cannot express the state of mind that a person experiences in that condition, but God understands. Just as He had been my "Helper" and "Comforter" so many times in the past, He came to me once again. He moved this mountain of despair at precisely twelve noon, a time when I could not help myself. He never left me; He was always there. It was a miracle of deliverance in which the faith that I held on to delivered me that day. God moved that mountain. Today, I can praise God for His rescue and can testify of His faithfulness. Faith does move mountains and what a difference He has made in my life.

God is interested in us walking with Him by faith. I tell you, whatever you pray for and ask, believe you have got it, and you shall have it (Mark 11:24).

Our struggles are real in the world of sin in which we live. During this experience of despair and hopelessness, I can honestly attest to the fact that although I prayed, I had moments of doubt and even questioned the presence of God. I tried rebuking my doubts and repeating affirmations of His faithfulness to me in the past, but at times I felt my voice wasn't being heard. God taught me many lessons that night and probably one that I will continually apply is the power of persistence in prayer calling on the Power within me. As a result of this experience in which God through the power of the Holy Spirit strengthened me, I will always be able to reflect on His faithfulness in my time of need. However, I believe He taught me that His presence is always with me regardless of the mountains I face.

Our Master's love gives us peace and comfort when everything around us seems to be raging in storms of despair. "The peace of God, which passes our understanding, will keep your hearts and your minds in Christ Jesus" (Phil. 4:7).

There is a story retold by Catherine Marshall in *The Helper* that was cherished by her husband, Peter. The story is descriptive of the peace that only God provides:

> *At one time a famous artists' association announced a contest. All pictures entered in the contest were to depict "peace." The winner would be awarded a large sum of money.*
>
> *Paintings of all sorts were submitted. There were serene pastoral scenes; placid lakes; an intimate cottage scene, cheerful and snug before a cozy fireplace; untrammeled vistas of freshly fallen snow; a painting of a tranquil, windless dawn in muted opalescent colors. But the painting selected by the judges for the first prize was very different from all the others. It depicted the height of a raging storm. Trees bent low under lashing wind*

and driving rain. Lightning zigzagged across a lowering, threatening sky. In the midst of the fury, the artist had painted a bird's nest in the crotch of a gigantic tree. There a mother bird spread her wings over her little brood, waiting serene and unruffled until the storm would pass. The painting was entitled very simply, Peace. (Marshal, 185)

Just as the mother bird spread her wings over her little brood, the embodiment of the Holy Spirit within us offers His protection with His peace and care to each of us. He just asks us to walk with Him in faith.

Everything in our experience with God depends on the quality of our relationship with Him. The one thing God wants from us is to love Him with all of our being. The Holy Spirit assures us of that love. In Romans 5:5, scripture says, "God's love has been poured out in our hearts through the Holy Spirit" (Amplified). His presence is in us, poured out into our hearts through "our" invitation at salvation. Then, He waits for us to draw from the resources of power available to us.

Recently, in a small group session in which I helped facilitate from Max Lucado's book, *Unshakable Hope*, I began to focus on the many promises he described as being in a "glistening jewelry box" of God's inheritance. As "heirs of God and co-heirs with Christ" (Rom. 8:17), we have all the spiritual resources available to us to be everything God desires and all we hope for to equip us both personally and spiritually. When will we learn that we have direct access to the power of an omnipotent God through spiritual resources that can transform our lives? (Lucado, 37).

Transformation in times of loneliness, desperation, affliction, and uncertainty, restoration can come if we will draw from the power of His resources. All we have to do is look around us to see people who are drowning under the waves of hopelessness and have drifted into the woes of their existence. They fail to recognize the One to whom they can call to give them hope. Instead, they look within themselves for solutions as they blame others for their sinking desperation. They look for other means of resolve to deaden their pain.

If only—if only they would be sensitive to the Holy Spirit as He calls their name and look up to the Power available to lift them up out of their mire of self-destruction, then they would find the hope and joy they desire. The quote from R. C. Sproul describes it this way: "The Spirit brings order out of chaos and beauty out of ugliness. He can transform a sin-blistered man into a paragon of virtue. The Spirit changes people. The Author of life is also the Transformer of life."

Another spiritual resource available through the Holy Spirit is intercessory prayer. There are times we come into the presence of God, our hearts are heavy, and we simply do not know how to pray. Fortunately, we can rely on the intercession of the Holy Spirit for personal discernment to reveal truths to us as we pray. He knows our needs and every heartfelt concern which we desire to communicate to God. "In the same way, the Spirit helps us in our weakness. We do not know what we ought to pray for, but the Spirit himself intercedes for us with groans that words cannot express" (Rom. 6:28, NIV).

God also allows us the ability to acquire wisdom in the study of scripture through the power of the Holy Spirit. Reading, study, and prayer over the inspired words of God provide us spiritual understanding as we receive inspiration and truth for application to our daily lives. There have been times in each of our lives when we have repeatedly read and studied scripture, not discerning its spiritual meaning. Yet reading that same scripture with the inspiration of the Holy Spirit's discernment of the heart of God, we experience understanding never known before. "The Spirit searches all things, even the deep things of God. For who among men knows the thoughts of a man except for the man's spirit within him? In the same way, no one knows the thoughts of God except the Spirit of God" (1 Cor. 2:11, NIV).

As we grow in the power of the Holy Spirit and focus on the available riches He provides, let us make an intentional effort to arise each morning in a personal relationship with Him. You might try what I have begun to practice as I recognize His abiding presence within me. I start my day, "Good morning, Holy Spirit. Fill me with the desires of Your heart that I might be used in some way to bring Glory to God and make Him smile." I have found that beginning my day with a focus on my need for total surrender allows me to draw on another spiritual resource—the power to be a witness of my faith.

To be molded into the masterpiece of God's design, we must recognize the power we possess as He abides within us, knowing there is nothing greater than His Presence.

Prayer

As we come before Your Holy throne of grace, help us to acknowledge the power that indwells us through Your presence in the Holy Spirit. Let us draw on Your strength in our weakness. Quiet our spirits and help us sense what You seek to say, what You would have us do, and what You would have us be in order to glorify Your name. Let Your Spirit illuminate us to reflect *Who* you are in us.

Transforming the Ordinary
to the Extraordinary

*B*ecoming a Masterpiece in the Potter's Hand requires us to be pliable in such a way to be used willfully as instruments to glorify God according to His purpose. The abiding presence of the Holy Spirit within us equips us to rely on heaven's power to be what only He can make possible within us, granting us His unlimited potential. Our ability is limited but with Him nothing is impossible. "Jesus looked at them and said, with man this is impossible, but with God all things are possible" (Matt. 19:26, NIV). With what God makes possible, He can transform us from the ordinary to the extraordinary vessels of His design as He pilots us through our life.

The same is true when we think of the presence of God to empower us in service. Is God your pilot or copilot in service for Him? Spiritually, we have a choice. We can allow Him to guide and direct our life as we give Him complete control, or we can choose to go through life handling every problem in our limited strength, only drawing from Him in times of desperation. Jesus wants to abide within us at all times rather than just be near as a copilot. If God pilots our life, He abides in us as the vine, the true vine, as expressed from the mouth of Jesus when He said, "Abide in me, and I in you. As the branch cannot have fruit of itself, except it abide in the vine; no more can ye, except ye abideth in me. I am the vine, ye [are] the branches: He that abideth in me and I in him, the same bringeth forth much fruit: for without me ye can do nothing" (John 15:4–5, KJV). God calls us to bear fruit in service for Him. He created us for service and desires that we have His passion for service. His passion came with a cost and was revealed in His redemptive, holy work for our salvation at the cross. Our love and gratitude for His sacrifice must reflect our total surrender. As our copilot, He can only empower us in service when we choose to relinquish our will to the One who desires to pilot our life.

Through His work in us, we can be transformed from ordinary to extraordinary to accomplish His purpose. When He abides in us, it should be our desire that our transformation will reflect our love for Jesus as it becomes evident in our eyes, our face, our hands, our heart, and our love for others.

Total transformation requires consecration of our mind, body, soul, spirit and will for His glory. Such surrender must encompass an understanding as in the eyes of a young child.

> *One Sunday morning while attending a church service, a young boy became confused about something the pastor had said in his sermon. When he saw the pastor in the parking lot, he ran up to him, tugged at his sleeve,*

and inquired respectfully, "Sir, can I ask you a question about your sermon?" The pastor graciously agreed on his way to the car and gave the young boy his full attention, "Sure, son, what is it?"

The boy explained, "You said I could ask Jesus to come into my heart."

"That's right," the pastor responded.

"But Jesus is a Man in a man's body," the little boy replied.

"That's right," the pastor patiently answered.

As a frown creased his brow, the youngster persisted, "But I'm just a little boy."

The pastor gravely nodded. "That's right."

The puzzled look on the young boy's face betrayed his total ignorance of the truth he was about to utter. "But if I'm just a little boy and Jesus is a Man, if He comes into me, He'll be sticking out all over."

"That's right," the pastor agreed with a knowing smile. Having Christ inside you pushes the character of Christ to the forefront

so that others see Jesus "sticking out all over"
us during those times.

Each of us also has an important decision to make just as this little boy. Will we allow God (through Jesus) come abide in us? If God pilots our life, He will be "sticking out all over" us. Hopefully, we will be so full of our love of Christ it will flow from the inside to the outside.

In 2 Timothy 1:9 (NIV), we are reminded that our actions should be reflected in our service for a holy life. "He has saved us and called us to a holy life—not because of anything we have done but because of his own purpose and grace." This holy life will be reflected by the fruit we bear as we exemplify a passion for ministry and service.

Fulfilling God's purpose in our life comes through His creation of us with differing gifts and talents. Each of us is unique with His divine purpose in mind for us. Through prayer and availability, He will enable us to make contributions that will glorify Him.

Not only has He created us with gifts for service, He has called us to serve. Too often He calls, but we fail to listen. He speaks to us through the Holy Spirit who gives us a passion for service. Whether we accept the call is a choice. Once we accept the call or passion for service, we will be enabled to serve with His power. Frequently, we use excuses for not serving, but usually our failure to serve is due to our selfish motives in which we put self first rather than allowing God to help us prioritize our life with His desires above our own.

"For we are God's masterpiece. He has created us anew in Christ Jesus, so we can do the good things he planned for us long ago" (Eph. 2:10, NLT). As God's masterpiece, we were uniquely molded and shaped for His service. Look around and pause, noticing the uniqueness of everything God created. His handiwork provided an intricacy of plant and animal life with their life-giving systems. Each of them was uniquely and creatively designed for a specific purpose. Watching animals, some that hop, run, swim, burrow, and others that fly, we watch with the astonishment of His hands. To watch a bird building a nest for its young, giving birth, and caring for the intimate needs of life without the use of a blueprint, observing the varied colors and characteristics of His creations, we can't help standing in awe and amazement at the wonder of the beauty He provides.

Just as He created them, He created us from the dust of the earth with abilities, interests, talents, gifts, personality, and life experiences from which to draw to give Him glory. When God made us, He made us distinctively different from every other creation with matchless capabilities. Obviously, He loved diversity and finds humor with our personalities—if you aren't sure of that, just look around you! He created each of us with a unique combination of traits. Even in marriage, opposites attract.

God made those who are shy and withdrawn, others who are sociable and outgoing; some who are detailed while others look at things globally, but each one brings balance and completeness to His purpose. God uses all of our differences to glorify Him, balancing our ministry and giving it some zest. How boring the world would be if we were all the same? Fortunately, we are noticeably diverse.

Our diversity is a blessing which He created to enhance our ministry opportunities. Being created in the image of God we are expected to serve others as Jesus did when He walked the earth. His example is a testimony of spiritual maturity and should be a role model for us as we touch the lives of others.

Although our personalities are different and these differences can be beneficial to meet the varied needs of others, it is important to know that we do not have a predisposition to serve. We find multiple excuses for not serving. We see ourselves as common, ordinary pottery that is flawed with sin and filled with weakness but if we look at the men in scripture, God used their weaknesses to glorify Him.

In *The Purpose Driven Life*, Rick Warren mentions the weaknesses of three biblical patriarchs that were used due to their weaknesses. God turned them into strengths with unlimited potential.

- Moses' temper was his weakness. In his anger, he murdered an Egyptian, struck a rock he was supposed to speak to, and broke the tablets of the Ten Commandments. Yet Moses was transformed into "a very humble man, more humble than anyone else on the face of the earth" as found in Numbers 12:3 (NIV).
- Low self-esteem and deep insecurities characterized Gideon's weaknesses, but God transformed

him into "a man of valor." "The Lord is with you, mighty warrior" (Judges 6:12, NIV).

- Abraham's fear was his obvious weakness. Twice, his fear resulted in him lying that his wife was his sister. In spite of his weakness, Abraham became known as "the father of those who have faith." "His word is in my heart like a fire, a fire shut up in my bones" (Jer. 20:9, NIV). (Warren, 275)

Just as these patriarchs' weaknesses were transformed into strengths, all God desires of us, is to be a servant with a heart of humility and availability. We serve a God who is greater than any comprehensible expectation. He just wants us to serve Him with all of our hearts and know that as He molds us, we are on the potter's wheel in the cradle of His hands. Once we become a pliable vessel, we can come humbly before God as a ready, obedient servant. Then He can take us and put us where He wills to accomplish His purposes.

The problem lies when we walk selfishly, guiding each path alone, sometimes stumbling in the dark of self-sufficiency, resisting the illumination of the power available to us to guide and direct our path. Self-seeking has no place in a Spirit-led life. To be servants, we must be obedient to the instruction of God and trust Him to accomplish it.

We often ask, "What can I, one ordinary person, do?" Excusing ourselves in claiming our limited ability to serve God, yet God loves taking ordinary vessels characterized by brokenness and flaws, transforming them into vessels with His specific purpose in mind. Seldom do we realize the impact we can make in the life of others if empowered by God's divine majesty. We need to stop looking at our life from worldly standards and look through the eyes of Jesus of what we can become.

To quote a godly orator, Delvin Atchison, the author of "Dreaming in League with God," he states, "We spend our lives in a mode of less than what we were meant to be. Our views of the divine possibilities for our mission in life are tainted by a prism of practical and possible. That is not the case with God. We serve a God that can ride chariots of a midnight hurricane and at the same time cross over the suspension bridge of a spider's web. We serve a God that holds oceans in the hollow of His hands and displays His omnipotence in a dewdrop. Each evening He takes light and matter, flings it against a canvas of darkness, hangs it across the horizon and it becomes the midnight sky. With God the amazing is an everyday occurrence. Our God can pull us up from the shackles of the mundane and reach the mountains of the impossible" (Atchison, 2017).

With the divine possibilities available to us to be on mission for God, why would we settle for less? Will our investments be in a career, a hobby, fame, or wealth? According to worldly standards, these are the gems of worth, but none of them will have lasting significance. I have found that the true meaning in life comes through being a servant who is humble, obedient, moldable, and available for the Master's use. When we go on mission for God, we are assured that we do not go alone. Instead, we will be equipped with a cache of gifts at our disposal through the manifestation of the Holy Spirit that indwells us. "But to each one is given the manifestation of the Spirit for the common good" (1 Cor. 12:7, NIV). The gifts given are varied and bestowed on us as an act of God's divine favor to equip us for a reason or purpose in our service to others. The ministries and their effects are intended to bear witness to the reality of Jesus.

God wants us to make a difference in the world in which we live. The only way we can make that difference is to allow Him to mold us from an ordinary piece of clay and make us into the finished product He chooses us to become.

A couple visited England in celebration of their twenty-fifth wedding anniversary. While they were there, they saw an antique store in which they chose to shop. Their love for antiques and pottery made them pause as their eyes caught sight of a beautiful teacup. They asked, "May we see that? We've never seen a cup quite so beautiful."

As the lady picked it up and handed it to them, suddenly it began to speak.

"You don't understand." It said, "I have not always been a teacup. There was a time when I was just a lump of red clay. My master took me and rolled me, pounded me, and patted me over and over and I yelled out, 'Don't do that. I don't like it! Let me alone,' but He only smiled, and gently said, 'Not yet!'

Then, WHAM! I was placed on a spinning wheel and suddenly I was spun around and around and around. 'Stop it! I'm getting so dizzy! I'm going to be sick!' I screamed.

"But the master only nodded and said quietly, 'Not yet.'

"He spun me and poked and prodded and bent me out of shape to suit himself and then...he put me in the oven. I never felt such heat. I yelled and knocked and pounded at the door.

"'Help! Get me out of here!'

"'Not yet.'

"When I thought I couldn't bear it another minute, the door opened. He carefully took me out and put me on the shelf, and I began to cool.

"Oh, that felt so good! 'Ah, this is much better,' I thought. But after I cooled, he picked me up, and he brushed and painted me all over. The fumes were horrible. 'Oh, please, stop it! Stop it!' I cried. He only shook his head and said, 'Not yet...'

"Then suddenly he put me back into the oven. Only it was not like the first time. This time it was twice as hot, and I just knew I would suffocate. I begged...I pleaded...I screamed...I cried...I was convinced I would never make it. I was ready to give up and just then the door opened, and he took me out and again placed me on the shelf, where I cooled and waited and waited, wondering, 'What's he going to do to me next?'

"An hour later, he handed me a mirror and said, 'Look at yourself.'

"And I did...I said, 'That's not me, that couldn't be me. It's beautiful. I'm beautiful!'

"Quietly he spoke: 'I want you to remember, then,' he said, 'I know it hurt to be rolled and pounded and patted, but had I just left you alone, you'd have dried up. I know it made you dizzy to spin around on the wheel, but if I had stopped, you would have crumbled.

"'I know it hurt and it was hot and disagreeable in the oven, but if I hadn't put you there, you would have cracked. I know the fumes were bad when I brushed and painted you all over, but if I hadn't done that, you

never would have hardened. You would not have had any color in your life.

"And if I hadn't put you back in that second oven, you wouldn't have survived for long because the hardness would not have held. Now you are a finished product. Now you are what I had in mind when I first began with you." (*The Potter and the Clay*)

Each of us also began as an ordinary lump of clay but are being molded in the hands of the Potter. We, too, can be transformed into an extraordinary vessel that He had in mind for us when we were first created. And even greater, He can receive the greatest glory! Truly, our life can be a masterpiece in the Potter's Hand.

Prayer

Help us, Father, to be molded into Your likeness working with You on Your mission to redeem a lost world. We pray that You will take us, just ordinary people, and do something extraordinary with the abiding presence of the Holy Spirit within us.

OUR LEGACY: A PASSION
FOR HOLINESS

*H*ave you ever given any thought to your legacy? Depending on the season of life you are in, you may not have given it too much consideration. For others, we, who are closer to the end than the beginning, think about the influence that our lives have on those we love. Yet it is never too early to recognize the impact our lives have on our family, friends, or associates.

Our greatest legacy is our life now, our influence, and our testimony. For fear that it may seem melancholy, we tend not to want to think of it, but we are building our legacy now in the way we live each day.

As we think about our children and grandchildren, what types of memories will be hidden deep in the recesses of their hearts in their remembrance of us? We want them to know how deeply we loved them, both in the things we said and didn't say, as well as those things we did which, as minor as it might have been, was a demonstration of our heartfelt love.

Will it be memories of those times we spent playing ball with them in the backyard, playing make-believe, the events we attended in support of them, or the encouragement we offered when things didn't just go as they hoped? For me, at least, it certainly would not consist of great wealth in the form of money or things, or anything I might have done that would leave any indelible mark on history.

In addition to the heartfelt love of a mother and grandmother, with the many special memories we shared, I would like to leave another inheritance that consists of those things that have eternal significance—investments in a passion for holiness. I want them to value God's Word with an emphasis on the gospel of divine grace and their need for a Savior. I want to leave a legacy that will affect them long after I am gone.

Have you ever noticed that those around us learn more from us by watching us live than by listening to what we say? In recent years, due to my service with homebound, I have attended many funerals or memorials celebrating life. Listening to the remembrances, I have reflected on my life as it ebbs away. I seriously have had moments in which I have paused and questioned, "What impact has my life really made?" I have to admit that during my younger years I never gave it any thought, but as I age, it becomes more important to me. I would like to believe that my children and grandchildren will be inspired somehow by how I lived my life. Although in retrospect, I realize the many mistakes that I have made, but I hope that they can learn from my mistakes, which will be lessons that can impact them in a positive way.

I love the quote from Charles Spurgeon in his book *A Passion for Holiness in a Believer's Life*, when he says, "We are not what we should be, we are not what we want to be;

we are not what we hope to be; we are not what we shall be; but we do love the name of the Lord and this is the root of the matter. We shall be like Him, for we love Him" (Spurgeon, 39).

Oh, how I hope that my life will reflect the desires of a heart for holiness and that others would see that I truly loved the Lord. "But just as He who called you is holy, so be holy in all you do; for it is written: Be holy, because I am holy" (1 Pet. 1:13–16, NIV). My sincere desire is to be holy as He is holy. Yet I have to give careful consideration to those areas in my life that could reflect my passion for holiness.

Will my passion for holiness reflect my love for God's Word? Will my children remember seeing me read the scriptures, making application to my daily life or see it as a ritual? "For the word of God is living and active, sharper than any double-edged sword, piercing until it divides soul and spirit, joints and marrow, as it judges the thoughts and purposes of the heart" (Heb. 4:12, ISV). Will they trust in the inerrant truth in the Word of God and when faced with the criticism of the Bible in college as they stand in classes of agnostics, will they stand strong in its defense?

Will my legacy leave an imprint on the hearts of my children or grandchildren in the power of prayer, praying unashamedly in the presence of others? Oh, how I hope my prayer life will leave an indelible picture etched in their hearts of the importance of a personal relationship with God, recognizing that when we pray, we are present in the throne room of heaven—not alone, but have Jesus and the Holy Spirit as our intercessors. Likewise, the Spirit also helps in our weaknesses. "For we do not know what we should pray for as we ought, but the Spirit himself makes intercession for us with groanings too deep for words. And he who searches hearts knows what is the mind of the Spirit, because the Spirit intercedes for the saints according to the will of God" (Rom. 8:26–27, ESV).

Will my desire for holiness be a legacy implanted on their hearts of the value I placed on worship, and the deep love I had for the Lord? Will they remember hearing me singing hymns both in church and as I sang them to sleep? Will they remember seeing the tears roll down my cheeks when the Holy Spirit spoke to me in a very personal way during a sermon?

What about the investment of time? From the time we were children, we placed an important emphasis on time. How we spent time was always something we thought about: looking forward to the summer away from school; becoming a teenager so we could drive; waiting for the time to be able to wear makeup, get pierced ears, or date. In our younger years, we wanted to hurry to fulfill hopes and dreams that our days of our youth delayed.

However, as years pass rapidly away and old age creeps in, we accentuate other areas of importance in our life— one of them being our time. Will our time be used for ourselves or an investment in the lives of others? God has given us the gift of life in minutes, hours, days, and years, and He expects us to use the opportunities He provides to serve Him. He wants us to make a difference in the world by working through us as His hands, feet, and mouth to touch the lives of others. Jesus wants us to continue what

He started—not only to come to him but to go for him. He doesn't want us in pieces, He wants our all and to share Him with all. Will we give Him less than our best?

> Will we give Him…
> our Sundays but not our Mondays.
> our actions but not our attitudes.
> our relationships but not our reputations.
> our time but not our thoughts.
> our burdens but not our bodies.
> our prayers but not our pleasures.
> our crises but not our children.
> our grief but not our goals.
> our health but not our hearts. (Lotz, 165)

The ways our lives become interwoven into the lives of others are often mysterious to us but not to God. There will be occasions in our life in the midst of the busyness of our schedule that we experience a sense of urgency to make a phone call or go on a visit which we cannot explain.

During those times, we often try to dismiss it, and at other times, it comes with such persistency that we cannot ignore it. From personal experiences, I have found that such urges result in being divine appointments in which God is using us as His messenger at a designated time with specific purpose.

On one particular occasion, I experienced the need to call a member in our church who was only an acquaintance. I felt a little uncomfortable about calling since I had no idea for what reason I was calling, but I trusted that God did.

This was not the first time that I had responded at God's direction. When she answered the phone, I told her who I was and readily told her I wasn't sure of the purpose for which I was calling but God had told me to call her.

She gasped and said, "Mary, I have just received some terrible news of the death of a close friend with small children and I am devastated by it." I asked for her friend's name and told her I would be praying for the family. She told me how much it meant to her that I had been sensitive to the voice God in her time of need.

God leaves a legacy through us through words of encouragement offered, through shared personal stories of answered prayers, and the needs He has met on our journeys in life. People who do not have a personal relationship with God often have misguided notions of His character. God wants to use us as an instrument of His heart. Everything we do in service for Him should come from a heart filled with compassion of His loving-kindness. Jeremiah 24:7 (NIV) says, "I will give them a heart to know me, that I am the LORD. They will be my people, and I will be their God, for they will return to me with all their heart." Our model for the legacy we leave should be founded on the love and self-sacrifice of Jesus.

Think about all the fascinating stories of how Jesus's love was shown through His interaction with people. There was Saul on the road to Damascus (Acts 9:1–15, KJV), the woman at the well (John 4:1–29, KJV), a despised tax collector (Matt. 9:9, KJV), to the thief on the cross (Luke 23:39–43). Wherever God led, they found the inspiration to follow. Each one of these meetings was orchestrated by a divine revelation from God. The designated time and place had an impact that transformed lives. His love and compassion for humanity is an example to each of us. It is through the major life lessons we can discern from Scripture of people Jesus encountered that has left us with a legacy of His holy passions.

In considering what our legacy will be, if we will be available and pliable in His hands, God will mold each of us into the image of His Son, Jesus, shaping us for a specific purpose. We will become a masterpiece that will help build His kingdom. As the Potter, He may subtract something from our life—similar to removing lumps from clay. Another possibility is that He may speed up the pace until we feel we are spinning. Or He might dramatically rework our pattern of living in order to start us in a different direction. Our responsibility is to accept any changes from the Master Potter as He forms the legacy He chooses us to leave.

If we desire to leave a legacy for our passion for holiness, we must be available and pliable in the hands of God. Through willing submission, we will be molded into the image of His Son as He shapes us for a specific purpose—to help build His kingdom. As the Potter, He may need to refine us, removing our brokenness and flaws from our life. Or He might dramatically rework our pattern of living in order to start us in a different direction. Our responsibility is to accept any changes from the Master Potter as He forms the legacy He chooses us to leave.

It has been said, "What matters is not the duration of our life, but the donation of it. Not how long we lived, but how we lived" (*Peter Marshall Quotes*). We are leaving a legacy whether we want to or not. What will it be? Our children, grandchildren, friends, acquaintances, coworkers, even people we do not know are watching and observing us—possibly, at times unaware to us.

Let us pray that our legacy will reflect our love of God with a passion for His holiness. Tony Evans so aptly puts it this way, "Your life is like a coin. You can spend it anyway you want, but only once. Make sure you invest it and don't waste it. Invest it in something that matters to you and matters for eternity" (*A Quote by Tony Evans*).

Let us pass it on. Let us pray that God will continue to work through our legacy to those we love and even those we may not know, throughout eternity.

Prayer

Father, let our legacy be one that is not only etched on our tombstone but one that will be etched in the hearts of those we love and have touched during our journey through life. Oh! How we should seek to make an eternal impact on others, especially our family.

THE JOURNEY TO CALVARY—
WERE YOU THERE?

Jesus said to His disciples, "If anyone desires to come after Me, let him deny himself, take up his cross, and follow Me" (Matt. 16:24, KJV).

Have you ever given much thought about the effect the cross has had on your life? The cross defines everything in our relationship to God if we are to be followers of Jesus. It means denying ourselves through the total surrender of every fiber of our being, abandoning self-centeredness for God-centeredness every moment of every day.

Carrying the cross is a vivid illustration of a moment-by-moment decision to take the same road of sacrifice and service that Jesus took. The road to the cross was long and grueling.

In order for us to adequately put the pieces together, and truly understand the whole picture of this divine event, we must refuse any prejudices and let God tell us what to believe. As we examine the biblical characters on the journey to Calvary, we must be cautious not to be judgmental along the way. Instead, examine the role we might have played had we been there.

Some of the biblical characters we would expect on the journey to Calvary with Jesus would be his disciples. These men were ordinary men whom God used in an extraordinary manner—fishermen, a tax collector, a political zealot, and other ordinary men. These were men that experienced the same failings, doubts, and struggles we do. They were prone to faults, mistakes, misstatements, bad attitudes, and lapses in faith. Yet it is from these men that we learn who Jesus is! As His witnesses, Jesus's words, actions, interactions, and His ultimate sacrifice for humanity were recorded.

Their absence is apparent as we look along the road to Calvary. Although they were all present in the Upper Room, the number of disciples dwindled when human weakness was derailed by the Evil One, and fear overcame them as Jesus announced of his upcoming death and resurrection.

On the evening of the Passover meal, news that one of them would betray Him confused the disciples. Each disciple hoped, yet wondered if they would have the courage to remain faithful. Although the other disciples were confused by Jesus's words, Judas knew their meaning. Judas, described by Jesus as the "son of perdition" (John 17:12), was a disciple whose name sends shudders up and down our spines. He was a successful hypocrite in the eyes of the other eleven disciples, judging him from all outward appearances. Few men had been trusted and blessed as Judas. He was with Jesus for three years and had special privileges, even as a trusted treasurer. Although Judas followed, he did so without ever giving his heart to Jesus. Judas lacked an authentic faith and Satan's counterfeit plan overpowered him that resulted in the betrayal of Jesus. Judas had been warned months prior to the betrayal. Jesus addressed him asking, "Did I Myself not choose you, the twelve, and yet one of you is a devil?" (John 6:70). Satan recognized the vulnerability of Judas and his weakness for money. Just as Satan used Judas, he can also tempt us to betray Jesus when he capitalizes on our human weaknesses—greed, power, control, or sensual pleasures. Although Judas experienced heart-wrenching remorse, he confessed it only to the priests and religious leaders: "I have sinned…for I have betrayed an innocent man." "What do we care?" (Matt. 27:4, NLT). After cutting a deal with the devil, he committed suicide, entering eternity, alone without a Savior.

We cringe when we think about the actions of Judas, but let us not be judgmental, especially, if at any time we, too, have claimed to be a follower of Jesus and lived a life of hypocrisy. Our hypocrisy is a sin of betrayal. Anne Lotz describes it this way: "You and I betray Jesus when we call ourselves Christian yet give our hearts to money, or material things, or selfish pursuits, or anyone or anything other than Him. We betray Him when we spend more time on the Internet than in prayer. We betray Him when we spend more time reading the morning newspaper than reading the Bible" (Lotz, 239).

Although Judas confessed his sin, he didn't confess it to the only One who has the power to forgive us from our sins. In 1 John 1:9, Jesus tells us, "If we confess our sins, he is faithful and just to forgive us our sins, and to cleanse us from all unrighteousness."

Following the betrayal of Judas, only eleven disciples remained, ten of which did not go the distance to Calvary. Only John, His most beloved disciple, traveled the gruesome distance to the cross but even then, there are no records of him saying anything in defense of Jesus. Would we have stood in his defense, or would we have hidden in the background?

Jesus knew the hearts of those with whom He spent his time. He knew their strengths and their weaknesses. He knew Judas would not be the only disciple that would be subject to the schemes of Satan that night during the Passover celebration. Jesus repeatedly warned the disciples of their upcoming unfaithfulness, but his words landed on deaf ears as they gathered in the Upper Room.

During his second attempt to warn the disciples of their upcoming denial and desertion, Jesus told them, "All of you will be made to stumble because of Me this night, for it is written: 'I will strike the Shepherd, And the sheep of the flock will be scattered'" (Matt. 26:31, NKJV). Jesus explained that they would deny any association with him and distance themselves from him.

As the disciples strongly disputed what Jesus said, Peter, the impetuous one, declared his loyalty would be stronger than the others. Yet he found that through his strongest efforts, he would inevitably have to look into the blood-drenched face of Jesus with His piercing eyes revealing his hypocrisy and sin. Peter immediately recalled the words He had been warned of earlier. Despite his best intentions, the promise he had initially made veered from assurance to his deep remorse of sin, followed by his humble confession to God. Peter learned that God's forgiveness surpasses every experience when we fail. Our talk is cheap. It is easy to say we are devoted to Christ, but our claims are meaningless if we cannot withstand the tests and temptations we often face. Temptations strike us when we are the most vulnerable.

After eating, the disciples went out to the Garden of Gethsemane. Jesus took his inner circle (Peter, James, and John) farther into the garden with him and revealed his innermost turmoil over the event he was about to face. As his horrible death and separation from the Father loomed over him, he asked Peter, James, and John to stay with him, keep watch, and pray. "My soul is overwhelmed with sorrow to the point of death. Stay here and keep watch with me" (Matt. 26:37–38, NIV). Three different times Jesus asked his beloved disciples to watch and pray with him. Each time, returning to find the disciples asleep. After spending much time in prayer, Jesus was ready to face all that he had predicted about his death.

The disciples learned a lesson that we, too, must learn. We are all flawed due to our sinful natures. We must confront the truth that no good thing dwells within us. It does not matter the size of our sin whether large or small. If we will only come to Him in a spirit of humility and with a heart of repentance, our Savior will grant us His grace and forgiveness.

How often opportunities are missed when we can spend time in prayer with our Father, yet we forsake that time for our distractions. The disciples had missed a great opportunity to talk to the Father and participate with him in his suffering and learned a valuable lesson—spiritual vigilance is a vital part of discipleship.

In our times of struggle, it takes firm trust in God with diligent prayer and obedience. If we are faithful in our obedience, we must stay off His throne. We must recognize our insufficiency and surrender our wills to Him daily.

After Jesus's betrayal in the garden, he was arrested. All the disciples deserted him and fled. Jesus faced six trials—three of them religious, three civil. Each one of them was illegal because they broke different components of Jewish law. Regardless of legality, the fate of Jesus was sealed, and he was ordered to be executed. He was scourged and crowned with thorns (Luke 22:63–65) and led out by four soldiers under the command of a centurion (Mark 15:39) to his execution. Like a condemned prisoner, Jesus was forced to carry the crossbeam of his cross, weighing about one hundred pounds on his already bleeding shoulders.

When Jesus took up His cross (John 19:17), He carried more than wood. He carried the weight of the sins of all of mankind—yours and mine, facing the punishment that these sins deserved. The burden of the cross on Jesus still speaks to us today to remind us that we, too, have a cross to bear. "Whoever does not take up their cross and follow Me is not worthy of Me" (Matt. 10:38, NIV).

Jesus started carrying His cross, but so weakened by the beatings He had endured, He was physically unable to carry it all the way to his execution site. The Roman soldiers had the authority to enlist others to assist in the needs they saw necessary which resulted in the calling of a passerby, Simon from Cyrene. Simon was traveling to Jerusalem for the Passover and had little to no knowledge of Jesus, yet was enlisted to carry His cross. How do you think he felt? Do you wonder how he must have felt as his journey to the Passover was interrupted? Called to carry a heavy crossbeam for a man he didn't know? Certainly, he was surprised and possibly annoyed, maybe even embarrassed, to be called upon to have an association with a criminal in the eyes of the Jewish religious leaders. But Simon was not given an opportunity to refuse as the soldiers "took hold" (Luke 23:26) of him, fearing that Jesus could not make it to the place of his execution due to the beating he had incurred. "After laying the cross on him, they made him carry it behind Jesus" (Luke 23:26). As Simon was forced to the ground under the weight of the cross, his eyes met the eyes of the innocent, humble Son of God through a disfigured face, with eyelids swollen shut, dripping with blood from the brutal scourging and beating He had endured. Can you imagine what it must have been like to look into His eyes through the "agony of love"? Did he see something in His eyes that revealed His divinity? Simon's heart must have been wrenched at such a sight. Yet Simon may have also been touched as he realized later that this opportunity was given to him as God's divine providence. God always blesses those who support His Son.

What thoughts must have gone through the heart of Jesus as He passed along the Via Dolorosa, carrying the burden of the world, watching those who sneered insults at Him, looking for His friends, disciples, or those whom He had performed miracles? I also wonder if the eyes of Jesus were filled with tears as He felt the abandonment of those He had grown to love.

Where were Lazarus, Martha, and their sister, Mary? Jesus had spent much of his final days with them. Were they fearful of the danger they would encounter if they stayed with Jesus? What about those whom Jesus had healed? Where were they?

Although Jesus must have felt He was going to the cross alone without many of those with whom He had intimate fellowship, He still forgave them and used them through their testimonies and service.

Outside the walls of Jerusalem was a limestone ridge, known as Calvary, or Golgotha, "the Place of the Skull." It was a common ground for crucifixion or extreme suffering. It was here that they crucified Jesus. Although it was a short journey to travel for One condemned to die, it was perilous for Jesus. A multitude of people had gathered for the crucifixion of Jesus for very different reasons:

- Crowds of people who were curiosity-seekers watched and scorned Jesus and found it a spectator sport. Some of these same revelers had previously shouted "Hosanna" and praises to God in honor of His entry. They had placed palms and branches as He entered Jerusalem on Palm Sunday in recognition of the many miracles He had performed.
- Enemies of Jesus rejoiced when the outcome of His trials resulted in His condemnation for the crime of blasphemy. They yelled, "Crucify him! Crucify him!" (Luke 23:21).
- Faithful to the end were the women who loved Jesus and gathered to mourn His crucifixion. They

wept bitterly as they remembered their deliverance from their past, and the hope He restored for their future. There was Mary Magdalene, from whom He had cast out demons (Mark 16:9); Mary, the mother of James and Jose (Mark 15:14); and Joanna and Salome, the mother of James and John (Luke 24:10). Let us not forget the love of Mary, the mother of Jesus. Can you imagine how her heart grieved for her as she watched His agony? Although she did not completely understand the purpose of His crucifixion, she stood at the foot of the cross and refused to abandon him.

- Roman soldiers stripped Jesus naked, dressed Him in a robe and crown, beat Him, mocked him, as well as gambled for His clothes (John 19:1–15; Luke 22:63; Matt. 27:35–37). Not only did Jesus suffer physically, but His spiritual suffering was even worse. As He bore the sins of the world, He was not only stripped of His physical clothes, He was "stripped of His robe of righteousness and exposed to His Father's penetrating gaze of searing holiness" (Lotz, 275). Did they not realize they crucified the Son of the most-high God?

- However, there was a Roman centurion who was probably overseeing Jesus's crucifixion who came to realize the depth of divinity found in Jesus. As he stood at the foot of the cross, consider what he must have seen, and every word Jesus spoke. Was it the words of Jesus when He said, "Father, forgive them, for they know not what they do"? (Luke

23:34). Or was it when Jesus showed mercy to the thief on the cross? Regardless of what created the Roman centurion to have a changed heart, it was reflected in the scripture from Luke 23:47 when "he glorified God, saying, certainly this was a righteous man."

- The two thieves, one on His right and the other on His left, faced two different fates (Luke 23:39–43, NIV). One thief hurled insults at Jesus saying, "Are You not the Christ? Save Yourself and us!" But the other answered, rebuking him said, "Do you not even fear God, since you are under the same sentence of condemnation? We indeed are suffering justly, for we are receiving what we deserve for our deeds; but this man has done nothing wrong." And the thief added, "Jesus, remember me when You come in Your kingdom!" And Jesus said to him, "Truly I say to you, today you shall be with Me in Paradise" (Luke 23:39–43). While our Lord experienced physical, emotional, and spiritual trauma at the cross, He still demonstrated His divine love for mankind. In the midst of His pain, He still listened compassionately to the pleas of a sinner.

- At the foot of the cross stood Mary, Jesus's mother, and John, His most beloved disciple. When Jesus saw them, He said, "Woman, behold your son." Then He said to the disciple, "Behold your mother." And from that hour, that disciple took her to his home (John 19:25–27).

- Joseph of Arimathea and Nicodemus, two men who had secretly believed in Jesus when He lived, now claimed His body for burial (Matt. 27:57–61; Mark 15:42–47; Luke 23:50–56; John 19:23, 24).

All those who were at the cross experienced sights and sounds by which you and I would be traumatized. When Jesus reached Calvary, He was made to lie with His head on the ground, and his arms outstretched on the wooden crossbeam. There must have been a pause in the jeers by the hecklers when the soldiers picked up the long spikes, possibly five to seven inches long, to secure him to the beams. Pause. Listen. Can you hear the moans from the pure agony Jesus felt when the spikes pierced through His wrists, tearing the skin as they were pounded into the wooden beams? The crossbeam was then lifted up with Jesus attached and fixed to the upright beam of wood. As if that had not been enough in addition to the beatings He had already endured, His knees were slightly flexed with His ankles overlapped, and the third spike nailed through both feet. Jesus was now crucified.

As we examine our hearts, where would we have been along the journey to the cross?

- Would we have been like the disciples when confronted in the Upper Room about their faithfulness, even to the point of denial?
- Would we have been a Judas who claimed to be a follower of Jesus but lived a life of hypocrisy

(claiming our spirituality and morality), unaware of our need for repentance?

- Or would we be like Peter, who declared a strong allegiance to Jesus without the understanding of the power of temptation, realizing we are "all broken" due to our sinful nature?
- Would we be more like the "inner circle" in the Garden of Gethsemane when asked to pray and share in the suffering of Jesus, yet our spiritual vigilance was lacking?
- Would we be like Simon, possibly annoyed or even embarrassed to help carry the cross that bears our sin? But later, after looking into the eyes of Jesus come under conviction of the cost being paid?
- Then there were the four soldiers who gambled for the clothes of Jesus. Would you have been there rolling the dice for his "robe of righteousness" through the belief that your righteousness can be earned or bought?
- Would you have found yourself as one of the thieves on the cross beside Jesus—one who tried to manipulate Jesus or the other who confessed his faith threw himself in the mercy of Jesus's grace?

Hopefully, we would have had the unconditional love of Mary, his mother, or the transforming love of the Roman centurion and the thief on the cross who recognized that Jesus was truly the Son of God.

I must admit that every time I study the journey to the cross, I am overwhelmed with guilt and humility. I sincerely question what role I might have played on this heart-breaking journey. Do you? I do know one thing for sure! I am unworthy of the price my Lord paid.

Regardless of the role, we might have played on the journey to the cross, we must remember we are still being shaped by His hands. Although we are weak vessels, we must trust God completely during our times of refinement and know we are in the Potter's Hands, being made into a masterpiece for His glory. "Yet, O LORD, You are our Father. We are the clay, You are the potter; we are all the work of Your hand" (Isa. 64:8).

Prayer

Our Father in heaven, we thank You for the mercy You extended to us for our sins that nailed You to that old rugged cross. Forgive us for the questions and even doubt that prevail when we question our faithfulness to You had we been along Your journey to the cross. Too often we are quick to judge those who denied and abandoned You, but we admit we fail You even today. We praise and worship You for the sacrifice You made on our behalf. Help us be mindful of our need to pick up our cross daily to show our love for You.

A Gift of Compassion
and Eternal Hope

There is a story entitled "The Day Philip Joined the Group" that was told by Reverend Harry H. Pritchett in a sermon that exemplifies the meaning of true compassion and eternal hope:

On a Sunday morning in a Sunday school class of eight-year-old children, there was a boy by the name of Philip. The third graders did not welcome Philip. Not just because he was a year older, but Philip was "different."

He had facial characteristics that were obvious manifestations of the fact that he suffered from Down's syndrome, a mental retardation condition.

One Sunday following Easter, his Sunday school teacher gathered some plastic eggs that pull apart in the middle and gave each one of them a plastic egg.

It was a beautiful spring day, and they were given the assignment to go outside and discover a symbol of "new life." They were to place the symbol, whether it was a seed, leaf, or another object, into the plastic egg.

Upon returning to the class, each child would have the opportunity to explain how the object represented "new life."

The youngsters gathered around, put the eggs on the table, and the teacher began to open them.

One child found a flower. All the children were touched by the lovely symbols of new life.

In another was a butterfly. "Beautiful," the girls exclaimed. And it's not always easy for an eight-year-old to say "beautiful."

Another egg was opened to reveal a rock. Some of the children laughed. (You know some children can be so cruel.)

"That's crazy!" one said. "A rock can't represent a 'new life'!"

A little boy spoke up claiming his example and said, "That's mine. I knew everybody would get flowers and butterflies and all that stuff, so I got a rock to be different."

Everyone laughed.

As the teacher opened the last one, she found it to be empty.

"That's not fair," someone said. "That's stupid," said another.

The teacher felt a tug on her shirt. It was Philip. Looking up, he said, "It's mine. I did do it. It's empty. My life is new because of that empty tomb."

The class fell silent.

From that day on, Philip was never looked at the same. They welcomed him. Whatever had made him "different" was never mentioned again.

With all the things found in Phillip's tiny, frail body, his family knew he didn't have long to live.

*On the day he was to be buried, those who
had treated Phillip as an outsider came to
understand the real meaning of death as they
marched up to the casket.*

*Nine children with their Sunday school
teacher placed their genuine gift of love
and an understanding of eternal hope—an
empty egg.* (Gray, 17)

No greater truth could have been expressed by Philip than when he said "new life" begins with an empty tomb—the symbol of sacrificial love, mercy, and grace.

How I praise God for the victory that came forth from the tomb! Although we think of the pain and agony of the cross, we can find hope and renewal from the tomb for it was there that all of our sins (denial, hypocrisy, guilt, self-sufficiency, and self-righteousness) were nailed to the cross—not just Jesus. But also, all the commandments we have broken, all the failures and hurts we have caused. Those nails held our sins, not only covered by the blood of Jesus but were totally removed.

Our sins have been taken away from us forever by the finished work of Christ at the cross. Those sins were buried in the grave. "We were buried therefore with him by baptism unto death, in order that, just as Christ was raised from the dead by the glory of the Father, we too might walk in newness of life" (Rom. 6:4, ESV).

You and I need those nails even today to remind us that we have been fastened to a new life, a changed life, a different life, that truly sets us free. "So, if the Son sets you free, you will be free indeed" (John 8:36).

Philip was described as "different" in the story by Rev. Pritchett. Hopefully, as people see who we are and what we are becoming, they will see a transformation of His resurrection power in our life and say we, too, are different.

The love demonstrated through the cross proves there is no greater evidence of God's abundant love and compassion for us in that He placed His Son on the cruel cross to die on our behalf. Through His compassion, Christ absorbed the full fury of His Father's wrath and our sin. "Because of the LORD's great love, we are not consumed, for his compassions never fail. They are new every morning; great is Your faithfulness" (Lam. 3:22–23, NIV). He did not fight for His rights to the throne where He rightly belonged. Instead, He "emptied himself, by taking the form of a servant, being born in the likeness of men" (Phil. 2:6–7). Just as Christ became a sacrifice for us, we must deny the old life, claiming the new life, the changed life He made possible through His crucifixion and resurrection.

Praise God the grave could not hold Him captive. He is alive. He is resurrected, and the same resurrection power that delivered Jesus from death to life is available to us. His resurrection is a source of transforming power in our lives daily. When we experience the "newness of life" through the resurrection of Jesus, His transforming power begins a life-changing process within us. That transformation has a close similarity with the change that occurs in novice musicians in an orchestra when they come under the direction of a gifted maestro. Our life under the great Maestro can also lead and direct us toward a perfect concerto. If we have any hope of experiencing the melodious sound in life, we must bump our life off of our self-centeredness and shift our focus from a me-centered life to a God-centered life.

Each of us experiences those times of difficulty when we become overwhelmed with agonizing pain from events and decisions we have made, allowing regrets to engulf us. I can quickly remember the heaviness that I have shouldered through the years of actions that I wish I could undo. I am plagued by the burdens of "what-ifs" and "if only," with those regrets that cause me grief, yet realize I can't change the past.

Looking as far back as fifty years ago during a time that was very grim and indecisive for me, I faced a choice urged by the Holy Spirit to speak, which I ignored. Have you ever been there?

What if I had listened and made the decisive opportunity to speak, would the outcome have been different? My father had been dismissed from a mental hospital for depression. My mother had shared with me that my dad was still depressed and had mentioned to her that had it not been for me, his only child, he would commit suicide.

That day will forever be etched into my memory. The pain and regrets still linger. If only…

I walked in one day from attending summer school in college and saw my father looking at himself in the mirror in our small home. As I stood there, I wanted to go tell him how much I loved him and that God loved him even more. I wanted to tell him how his thoughts of suicide would devastate me and our family. I hesitated, not listening to the Holy Spirit as He spoke to me.

Within the next several months, I graduated from college, began teaching, got married to the love of my life, and then the call came. My father had put an end to his life.

What if...there wasn't a second chance? Not another opportunity to change the past. The pain, the regrets have taught me lessons that I will forever remember. Opportunities arise for each of us, choices have to be made, but the urging of the Holy Spirit cannot be ignored. Our grief and guilt can destroy what God intends for us in life. The pain we experience can be used to glorify Him. Embracing God's promises of unconditional forgiveness and love can ease the torment we feel. When I finally understood His compassion, I began to rely on His resurrection power to get me through the pain, guilt, and anguish I've felt and trusted in His grace. Hopefully, I can be an instrument of encouragement to others to listen and obey.

It is only through God's love and compassion that we are equipped to be victorious over the storms of life through which we must travel. "Because of the LORD's great love, we are not consumed, for His compassions never fail. They are new every morning; great is Your faithfulness" (Lam. 3:22–23, NIV). His resurrection empowers us with an anointing that enables us to do those things that may be difficult and challenging.

I believe that each one of us has a calling on our life. Yet not everyone does what they are called to do in life. Many times, we get distracted by other issues or pursuits and get overwhelmed by a task that feels too big to handle, or even get caught up in the emotions that distract us from God's will at that moment.

Whatever the reason for us getting off track, our lack of sensitivity to the Holy Spirit can be the root of it. We must realize it is His anointing, or resurrection power that will enable us to fulfill the work He calls us to do. This can occur only if we seek and cultivate a personal, intimate relationship with God, first and foremost. In so doing, He will anoint and enable us to do what He calls us to do with our lives, regardless of fear or even hesitation.

God decides when and how to use us as His vessels. Our part is simple—to be available. Our part is to realize and understand that we are anointed. Everyone is anointed with something, called to do something. First John 2:20 says, "You have been anointed by the Holy One." You and I have to believe that! From time to time, maybe we should look into the mirror and say, "I am anointed with His redeeming power!" Through His love and compassion, "nothing will be impossible with God" (Luke 1:37).

His resurrection not only demonstrates His love and compassion, but also eternal hope. His resurrection power guards our lives every day without fear of the challenges we may face tomorrow. Regardless of the pains, disappointments, and heartbreaking events we face, our eternal hope is secure. Although we may not know what the future holds, we do know Who holds our future.

We can be assured as sung by Keith and Kristyn Getty in their song, "In Christ Alone," He is our eternal hope:

> In Christ alone, my hope is found;
> He is my light, my strength, my song;
> This cornerstone, this solid ground,
> Firm through the fiercest drought and storm.
> What heights of love, what depths of peace,
> When fears are stilled, when strivings cease!
> My comforter, my all in all—
> Here in the love of Christ, I stand.
> (Keith Getty, Stuart Townend)

With the gift of compassion, love, and eternal hope Christ has granted to us, we have the responsibility of sharing it with others. Will others see the "newness in life" reflected in us due to the power of the resurrection and the transforming hands of the Master?

In our opening story, Philip's example of "new life" was demonstrated by an empty egg, symbolizing the empty tomb. In the eyes of his peers, he truly was "different." Not from the perspective of his physical appearance but from his spiritual revelation of the compassion and eternal hope made possible through the resurrection.

The compassion of Jesus and His love for us through the resurrection gives us an eternal hope of what is yet to come. Ortberg shared a story that adequately illustrates an explanation of a mind focused on hope.

> *It was a story about a woman who had been diagnosed with cancer and had been given three months to live. Her doctor told her to make preparations to die, so she contacted her pastor and told him how she wanted things arranged for her funeral service—which songs that she wanted to be sung, what scriptures should be read, what words should be spoken—and what she wanted to be buried with her favorite Bible.*

> *But before he left, she called out to him, "One more thing."*

> *"What?"*

> *"This is important. I want to be buried with a fork in my right hand."*

> *The pastor did not know what to say. No one had ever made such a request before.*

> *So she explained. "In all my years going to church functions, whenever food was involved, my favorite part was whenever food was involved, my favorite part was when whoever was cleaning dishes of the*

main course would lean over and say, 'You can keep your fork.' It was my favorite part because I knew that it meant something great was coming. It wasn't Jell-O. It was something with substance—cake or pie— biblical food.

"So I just want people to see me there in my casket with a fork in my hand, and I want them to wonder, What's with the fork? Then I want you to tell them, 'Something better is coming. Keep your fork.'"

The pastor explained that this woman, their friend wanted them to know that for her— or anyone who dies in Christ—this is not a day of defeat. It is a day of celebration. The real party is just starting. Something better is coming. (Ortberg, 169, 170)

The empty tomb has a message for us that whenever we are in the pits of despair or discouraged, the empty tomb is a symbol of our hope, reminding us to "keep our fork."

Prayer

Lord, thank You for Your gift of compassion, love, and eternal hope. Help us to remember our life is not about us. Although we experience tragedy, pain, and regrets, Your sacrificial forgiveness is sufficient for every need. Use our experiences to testify of the "newness of life" that has transformed us into anointed vessels that are viable in the hands of the Potter so that we, too, are different. May our life of compassion and love for You remind our family and friends that in our final days there is no reason for sorrow because we can look forward to the eternal hope of something better is yet to come.

THE FINAL PORTRAIT:
THE COLORS OF OUR LIFE

One night when Robert Louis Stephenson was a small boy, his nanny called him to come to bed. Due to his distraction he was oblivious to her summons. He was staring at something outside his nursery window. His nanny walked over, stood at his shoulder, and inquired patiently, "Robert, what are you looking at?" The little boy, without taking his eyes away from the window, exclaimed in wonder as he pointed to the lamplighter who was lighting the streetlamps, "Look, Nanny! The man is putting holes in the darkness!"
(Lotz, 18)

Just as the lamplighter put holes in the darkness, God's love poked holes in our darkness and replaced it with His light. He replaced our fear with His security, and our despair with His eternal hope.

The transformation process, although gradual, progresses from internal to external. "We must let the world see God illuminated through our lives that they will be drawn to the God we see" (Blackaby and King, 223). "You are the light of the world. A town built on a hill cannot be hidden. Neither do people light a lamp and put it under a bowl. Instead they put it on its stand and it gives light to everyone in the house. In the same way, let your light shine before others, that they may see Your good deeds and glorify Your Father in heaven" (Matt. 5:14–16, NIV).

If God were to paint our portrait today, what would it reflect? Portraits are effective and compelling when they tell us something about a person. A good portrait is not just a visual representation of a person. It also reveals something about the essence of the person. An artist may choose to depict the person exactly as they are—flaws included. Artists may also exaggerate a person's characteristics, whether good or bad. Conversely, the artist might kindly overlook the flaws, correcting imperfections and presenting an idealized view of the person.

What better Artist can there be than the Creator! He knows our flaws, brokenness, and the transformation that has changed us. He understands our spiritual journey we have traveled and the path we are on today. As He paints us, He knows the colors on the canvas of our life—the truth and changing reality.

For our purpose, the colors of our life are represented by the process of our spiritual growth along the way. These colors include many of the shades of the rainbow—silver, orange, pink, lavender, black, red, white, and gold, to name only a few.

Our journey is not without challenges and circumstances that test our faith, joy, and peace. I imagine He stands back as He gazes at the canvas, reflecting on our spiritual journey. He reflects to the past at our earliest creation and what we looked like in our mother's womb before we took our first breath. He remembers our first steps and the number of times we stumbled and fell, not only as a toddler but throughout our life.

With careful contemplation and a casual glance at the Book of Life, God begins an *abstract* piece of art that describes the fundamental changes He has seen taking place in our life.

Abstract, I questioned? After I carefully pondered the reason, God revealed to me that there are incomprehensible truths which relate to our understanding of the omniscience and omnipotence of our Father. He not only created all things, but He also preplanned everything that would happen in his Creation. He knows everything that has happened and everything that is yet to occur in the future. He is sovereign over all. Yet we still have the freedom with the choices we make, and they will genuinely affect the rest of our life. God knows specifically what our future holds, but for our purposes, we will only see what He chooses to reveal. Let us get a glimpse of the colors which have spiritual meaning from the Bible as reflected in the possible journey of our life.

As God begins to paint the colors of our life, He focuses on those times we can remember in our spiritual walk. He shades in our background with contrasting colors of silver. The darker shades of silver indicate the *spiritual nature of our battles* with Satan and his tactics of deception. Yet our Master's brush strokes add depth to the reality of His *refin-*

ing process as He shades the darker silver with a lighter texture that glistens as our future hope shines through.

With His hands, He then frames our portrait with a boundary of orange strokes that symbolize His strength in battle, equipping us to be the *warriors* that will find victory in His name.

With a splash of pink, the Potter's Hand blends the softer tints as He illustrates the process of total surrender with *humility*. There are people in our lives that leave an indelible impression on us due to their character, especially their humility (*What the Colors of God Represent in the Bible*).

Recently, I read an account of a man who preached to over 215 million people in person and hundreds of millions of others through media. When asked what might be said about him at his funeral, he replied that he hoped his name would not be mentioned. "I only hope that the name of the Lord Jesus be lifted up." Billy Graham was ninety-four at the time. He had filled stadiums on every continent and advised every US president from Truman to Obama. Yet his humility exemplifies the example of which we should strive to become. He realized how big God is and how small we are (*Unshakable*, 67).

As He envisions us on our knees under the convicting power of the Holy Spirit, He highlights the canvas with the softness of lavender as we lift our voices to heaven as we *stand in His presence*.

Standing in the presence of our righteous God, we are reminded of His holiness and see what our judgment should have been, had it not been for the gift of His Son. The absence of light which we once knew was symbolized by shades of black, representing the judgment of sin and death from which we were rescued. "For the wages of sin is death; but the gift of God is eternal life through Jesus Christ our Lord" (Rom. 6:23).

As the Father continues to paint our portrait, we see splatters of red, as if drops of Jesus's blood, for our atonement and redemption. His blood paid the ultimate sacrifice and washed us clean. Jesus is our life-line to eternal life. The blood He shed on the cross covered all of our sins—past, present, and future. "The cross *defines* everything else in our relationship to God, and it *releases* everything else in your relationship to God" (Blackaby, *Experiencing*, 75). Through God's grace and power, He has provided everything we need to live a holy life.

With the shedding of His blood, righteousness was made possible to us as we come to Him in faith. He washes us clean, white as snow. "Though your sins be as scarlet, they shall be as white as snow; though they be red like crimson, they shall be as wool" (Isa. 1:18). As a reflection of what we shall become, our portrait shines with a spectrum of His light. Although a lifelong process, we can become more like Him as He transforms us from the inside out.

The finishing touches are put on our portrait in rays of gold. With the color of gold, we reflect that our spiritual journey has taken us from darkness to light, fear to security, and despair to hope. God's love is more precious than the riches that the world could ever satisfy: "their silver and their gold shall not be able to deliver them in the day of the wrath of the Lord; they [silver and gold] shall not satisfy their souls" (Ezek. 7:19) (*Colors in the Bible*, 2–4, 7)

As God paints our final portrait, let us pray that the colors of our life will reflect who God says we are and what we can become through His grace and power. To be a masterpiece of His design, it should be our heart's desire that when people see us, they will not be able to tell where Jesus ends and we begin. Personally, I can say, "He is my anchor and I am secure in the shadow of the cross. For He is worthy!"

> Worthy of worship,
> worthy of praise,
> worthy of honor and glory;
> worthy of all the glad songs we can sing,
> worthy of all the offerings we can bring.
>
> You are worthy Father, Creator,
> You are worthy, Savior, Sustainer,
> You are worthy, worthy and wonderful,
> worthy of worship, and praise.
> (Hal Leonard and Shawnee Press Choral)

Prayer

Father, we want to thank You for the encounters we have experienced as we have journeyed through life. Help our lives demonstrate the attributes that will reflect You as we draw on the spiritual resources we have available to us through the indwelling of the Holy Spirit. Manifest yourself through us that we will become a masterpiece in the Potter's Hand. May you be glorified. Amen.

REFERENCES

"A Quote by Tony Evans." *Goodreads*, Goodreads, www. goodreads.com/quotes/8763681-your-life-is-like-a-coin-you-can-spend-it.

Atchison, Delvin. "Dreaming in League with God." Deacon Banquet, Bryan, TX. 11 Dec. 2017. Keynote Address.

Blackaby, Henry. *Experiencing the Cross: Your Greatest Opportunity for Victory over Sin*. Multnomah Books, 2005.

Blackaby, Henry T. *Experiencing God: Knowing and Doing the Will of God*. Broadman & Holman Publishers, 2008.

Cole, S. J. "Felling the Giants in Your Life." *Lesson 2: Felling The Giants In Your Life (1 Samuel 17) | Bible. org*, Related Media, 9 Sept. 2013, bible.org/seriespage/lesson-2-felling-giants-your-life-1-samuel-17.

"Colors in the Bible." *Reasons for Hope* Jesus*, 25 Jan. 2018, reasonsforhopejesus.com/the-meaning-of-colors-in-the-bible/.

Fairchild, Mary. "Why Is the Holy Spirit the Least Understood Member of the Trinity?" *ThoughtCo*, ThoughtCo, 27 Dec. 2018, www.thoughtco.com/who-is-the-holy-spirit-701504.

"Five Smooth Stones of: Faith, Obedience, Service Prayer, and Holy Ghost." *Five Smooth Stones of: Faith, Obedience, Service, Prayer, and Holy Ghost*, www2.byui.edu/Presentations/transcripts/devotionals/2001_07_10_mcgary.htm.

Gibbs, Nancy B. "Inspirational Stories." *Be Still with God*, www.sermonillustrator.org/illustrator/sermon5/be_still_with_god.htm.

Gregory, Joel. "Were You There?" Holy Week, Bryan, TX. 16 Apr. 2019. Bible Study.

gospelweb.net. *Buy The Milk—Inspiring Story about How God Supplies the Need of His Own.*, 26 Aug. 2009, www.gospelweb.net/Illustrations/BuyTheMilk.htm.

Grenbec, R. "Carrying The Cross with Simon Of Cyrene, by Richard Grenbec." *Homiletic & Pastoral Review*, 13 Apr. 2014.

"Inspirational Christian Connection." *Inspirational Christian Stories & Godly Short Stories*, www.gateway-tojesus.com/inspirationalstoriespage2.html.

Keith Getty, Stuart Townend. "In Christ Alone." Thankyou Music, 2002. Songs@integritymusic.com.

Laurie, G. "Facing Your Giants—Topical Studies." *Bible Study Tools*, Topical Studies, 21 Mar. 2011, www.bible-studytools.com/bible-study/topical-studies/facing-giants-11652635.html.

Lotz, Anne Graham. *Just Give Me Jesus*. W Pub. Group, 2000.

Lucado, Max. *Unshakable Hope: Building Our Lives on the Promises of God: Study Guide: Twelve Sessions*. Thomas Nelson, 2018.

Marshall, C. *The Helper*. Chosen Books, 1978.

McGary, Stephen. "Five Smooth Stones of Faith, Obedience, Service Prayer, and Holy Ghost." *Five Smooth Stones of: Faith, Obedience, Service, Prayer, and Holy Ghost*, 10 July 2001, www2.byui.edu/Presentations/transcripts/devotionals/2001_07_10_mcgary.htm.

Ortberg, John. *If You Want to Walk on the Water You've Got to Get out of the Boat*. Zondervan, 2001.

Packer, J. J. *Knowing God*. Intervarsity, 1993. *PEOPLE AT THE CROSS 14 People at the Cross*. www.biblecourses.com/English/downloads/pdfs/gifted/14-People.pdf.

"Peter Marshall Quotes." *BrainyQuote*, Xplore, www.brainyquote.com/quotes/peter_marshall_382640.

Sproul, R. C. "Azquotes.org." *AZquotes (Azquotes.org)— AZquotes*, updates.easycounter.com/azquotes.org.

Spurgeon, C. H., and Robert Hall. *A Passion for Holiness in a Believer's Life*. Emerald Books, 1994.

Stanley, Charles. *How to Listen to God by Charles Stanley*. Thomas Nelson, 1985.

Stanley, Charles F. *Living the Extraordinary Life: Nine Principles to Discover It*. Thomas Nelson, 2005.

Terry York, Mark Blankenship. "Worthy of Worship." Van Press, Inc./McKinney Music, Inc., 1988. www.music-services.org.

"The Potter and the Clay." *Spiritual*, 18 Feb. 2017, www.spiritual-short-stories.com/spiritual-short-story-67-the-potter-and-the-clay/.

Warren, Rick. *The Purpose Driven Life: What on Earth Am I Here for, Rick Warren*. Zondervan, 2007.

"What the Colors of God Represent in the Bible." *Christian Banners and Flags for Praise and Worship—Custom Made Praise and Worship Banners and Flags*, bannersfortheshepherd.com/bfts.asp? keyword=Colors.

ABOUT THE AUTHOR

*M*ary White lives in Texas with her husband and three dogs. She was a longtime educator in Tennessee and Alabama. She received her doctorate in educational leadership from the University of Alabama. Before she started writing, she was a classroom teacher, a middle-school principal, and educational consultant, traveling nationally and internationally.

In addition to her educational endeavors, one of her greatest joys has been making memories with her family: two sons, her daughter-in-law, and four grandchildren.

Her desire to write was inspired by the Holy Spirit to share a story of her spiritual transformation in the hands of God.

CPSIA information can be obtained
at www.ICGtesting.com
Printed in the USA
LVHW041244101220
673819LV00019B/434

9 781646 707805